Life Lessons from Psychological Science

UNDERSTANDING AND IMPROVING INTERPERSONAL DYNAMICS

Life Lessons from Psychological Science

UNDERSTANDING AND IMPROVING INTERPERSONAL DYNAMICS

FIRST EDITION

E. Scott Geller

Virginia Tech

cognella®

SAN DIEGO

Bassim Hamadeh, CEO and Publisher
Clare Kennedy, Associate Acquisitions Editor
Tony Paese, Project Editor
Christian Berk, Production Editor
George V. Wills, Illustrator
Jordan S. Oliver, Word-Processing Support
Jess Estrella, Senior Graphic Designer
Trey Soto, Licensing Coordinator
Natalie Piccotti, Director of Marketing
Kassie Graves, Vice President of Editorial
Jamie Giganti, Director of Academic Publishing

Cover image copyright © 2011 Depositphotos/monkeybusiness.
        copyright © 2013 Depositphotos/creatista.
        copyright © 2013 Depositphotos/Success_ER.
        copyright © 2019 Depositphotos/kolapatha@outlook.co.th.
        copyright © 2019 Depositphotos/Syda_Productions.

Printed in the United States of America.

cognella® | ACADEMIC PUBLISHING
3970 Sorrento Valley Blvd., Ste. 500, San Diego, CA 92121

CONTENTS

vi   **CONTENTS**

PREFACE

For more than 50 years I have studied, taught, and researched the science of human experience. This journey has made me realize the utmost value of applying particular evidence-based life lessons to improve interpersonal dynamics. I designed this manual to teach these 50 critical life lessons and inspire related teaching/learning conversations among diverse groups of individuals of all ages—anyone interested in applying psychological science to enrich personal and interpersonal well-being.

This manual can help you understand, appreciate, and enrich the human dynamics of everyday life. The focus is on understanding, appreciating, and improving situations involving human behavior, from educational settings and the workplace to the home—all aspects of life we encounter daily. I hope you will use this manual to engage students, employees, and family members in teaching/learning conversations about the psychology of health, safety, relationship-building, and life satisfaction. For example, ask this question to participants in a discussion group: Which life lessons could we apply to cultivate a brother's/sister's keeper culture of safe and satisfied students, employees, friends, or family members?

If understood and applied routinely and extensively, the life lessons elucidated in this manual would most assuredly enhance human welfare and well-being. Interpersonal conflict and bullying would be reduced. Work productivity, environmental conservation, and life satisfaction would be enhanced. People would feel more empathy and show more **compassion** toward others, and they would perform more intentional acts of kindness. We refer to such behavior as actively caring for people (AC4P)—www.ac4p.org.

Several life lessons reflect the behavioral-science principles of positive versus negative reinforcement, observational learning, and **behavior-based feedback**. Other life lessons reflect **humanism**, including empathy, interdependence, systems thinking, and self-transcendence.

A number of other life lessons are derived from social psychology, including six principles of social influence, the dynamics of group decision-making, and critical distinctions between discrimination and stereotyping. The research foundation of other life lessons reflect additional domains of psychological science, including sensation and perception, personality, health and stress, learning, and human motivation.

I hope you are encouraged by the potential large-scale applications of this manual as a tool to activate constructive teaching/learning conversations among diverse groups of individuals of all ages—anyone interested in learning how human dynamics can enhance personal and interpersonal well-being.

A LifeCOACH Manual

I refer to this scholarship as a "LifeCOACH" manual. The principles of psychological science revealed and explicated here connect directly to everyday life—the science of human experience. Interpersonal coaching is one sure way to apply these life lessons for the benefit of interpersonal dynamics and human well-being. But why are the letters of coach capitalized?

COACH represents an interpersonal sequence of events relevant for applying a particular life lesson (e.g., feedback, praise, observational learning, systems thinking, empathy, empowerment, or a social-influence technique) to improve the behavior of oneself and others.

The coaching process begins with **C**are. This is not a "gotcha" process focused on finding faults or mistakes in other people. It's an AC4P process. People acknowledge and support the desirable behavior of others and strategically point out opportunities for continuous improvement.

"When you know I care, you will care what I know. In fact, I care so much I'm willing to observe your behavior—with your permission of course—and offer useful behavior-focused feedback." This quotation reflects the critical **O**bserve phase of *AC4P coaching*. Sometimes a behavioral checklist is used to look for certain desirable and undesirable behaviors, as well as the environmental determinants of those observed behaviors.

Whether checklist-assisted or not, the objective is to **A**nalyze the ongoing interaction of specific behaviors and the environmental conditions that facilitate or inhibit those behaviors. These observations and interpretations are shared with the individual observed in the next step of AC4P coaching—**C**ommunicate.

Behavior can only improve with behavior-based feedback, and this occurs during the **C**ommunicate phase of AC4P coaching. Appreciation and acceptance of supportive and corrective feedback depend on appropriate delivery of the behavioral feedback.

If the person observed perceives the **C**ommunicate phase to be constructive, the last letter of COACH reflects the outcome—**H**elp. Effective behavior-based AC4P coaching helps people improve at a targeted task, whether the focus is health, safety, security, production, instruction, research, scholarship, or athletics.

Note that the AC4P coaching process benefits both the observer and the person observed. The individual observed learns certain behaviors to continue and/or discontinue. But the act of pinpointing those behaviors instructs and motivates related behavior of the AC4P coach. When AC4P coaches hold people they observe accountable to do their best, the coaches in turn develop self-accountability and *self-persuasion* to follow their own advice (Life Lessons 17, 18, & 19).

The more people who coach each other effectively, the greater the potential to achieve an AC4P culture in an organization, educational facility, or within a family. When the mission and behavioral objectives target human health, safety, welfare, and/or security, the process supports the achievement of an AC4P culture. Indeed, cultivating an AC4P brother's/sister's keeper culture depends on increasing the quantity and improving the quality of interpersonal AC4P coaching for the safety, health, success, security, and well-being of oneself and others. This LifeCOACH manual will show you how to make that happen by understanding and improving interpersonal dynamics.

INTRODUCTION

This is not a typical textbook or self-help manual. Rather, it is a primer for developing self-awareness and insight through engaging people in interpersonal conversation. Instructive and entertaining illustrations are provided for each of the 50 life lessons relevant to enriching an individual's life, along with related discussion questions to initiate interpersonal and intrapersonal (i.e., self-talk) communication about each life lesson.

Activating Interest in Psychology

The illustrations and explanations for the life lessons in this LifeCOACH manual were created to attract attention and interest in psychology—the science of human experience. Thus, this scholarship could be used by middle schools, high schools, colleges, and universities to introduce students to psychological science and promote interest in taking an introduction to psychology course.

A Supplement for a Large-Lecture Class

At several colleges and universities, the introduction to psychology course is taught in a large lecture class with minimal opportunity for students to get involved in the course content, beyond taking notes from lectures and reading an assigned textbook in order to perform well on a multiple choice exam. This LifeCOACH manual could be used in these classes to engage the students in interpersonal conversation and relevant cooperative learning beyond the classroom. The instructor could prompt out-of-class discussions of particular life lessons (related to assigned readings in the textbook) and subsequently review the relevant life lessons in class, along with a PowerPoint display of the workbook illustrations.

A Recitation Manual

Some high schools, colleges, and universities supplement their lecture presentations of introductory psychology with weekly or biweekly recitation sessions or discussion groups. For these situations, this LifeCOACH manual is an ideal tool. Indeed, this scholarship was designed to inspire constructive one-to-one and group discussions about psychological science, particularly research-based concepts from learning, motivation, perception, social psychology, leadership, applied behavioral science, psychological health, cognition, and decision-making.

Thus, many if not most of the topic domains covered in an introductory psychology course are integrated among the 50 life lessons of this potential recitation manual, but with a focus on applications to improve life satisfaction and human well-being. An instructor or discussion leader might select a psychology topic to discuss and then select the particular life lessons that relate to the particular discussion topic.

Beyond Introductory Psychology

While the obvious application of this LifeCOACH manual is for an introductory psychology course, this scholarship is relevant to supplement other psychology courses, especially classes that address real-world applications of psychological science. For example, this manual is ideal for a course in applied psychology, but unfortunately this is not a common course at colleges and universities. However, it is hoped that this scholarship will increase interest in offering classes in applied psychology.

Social psychology is offered at most colleges and universities, and many of the life lessons illustrated and explained in this LifeCOACH manual are derived from social psychology, including six social-influence principles, attributional bias, varieties of interpersonal conversation, social justice, cognitive dissonance, transformational leadership, groupthink, group decision-making, discrimination versus stereotyping, interpersonal attraction, social acceptance, descriptive versus injunctive norms, and an independent (individualistic) versus an interdependent (collectivistic) culture. Thus, this LifeCOACH manual could be used to engage students in a variety of teaching/learning conversations about key topics in social psychology.

Humanistic Behaviorism

Several life lessons in this LifeCOACH manual reflect an integration of concepts from humanism (e.g., empathy, self-motivation, self-transcendence) and behaviorism (e.g., selection by consequences, feedback, success seeking versus failure avoiding), and thereby these life lessons revive a popular academic term from the 1970s—*humanistic behaviorism*.

While this beneficial combination of principles from behaviorism and humanism might not suggest a particular college or university course, a workbook that shows value in using select principles of humanism (e.g., empathy) to make an application of behavioral science (e.g., corrective feedback) more effective should be of special interest to teachers of various psychology courses beyond an introductory psychology course—from classes in applied behavioral science and community psychology to courses that address health psychology, psychotherapy, and interpersonal counseling.

How to Use This LifeCOACH Manual

This LifeCOACH manual was designed to promote positive teaching/learning conversations and beneficial real-world applications. Here's an optimal way to use this manual: A group leader reads the page opposite the illustration for a particular life lesson and then facilitates a discussion about that life lesson. Questions and topics for discussion are presented with each illustration and following the one-page research foundation of each life lesson. However, additional questions and issues will likely evolve from a group discussion.

The size of the discussion group can vary from two to 30 or more. Constructive teaching/learning conversations about the life lessons can occur between two individuals or among the participants in a school classroom or at a corporate workshop led by a teacher or facilitator.

Discussion groups or recitation sessions for introductory psychology classes in high school, community colleges, or universities are the most obvious applications for this LifeCOACH manual. But select life lessons can facilitate critical discussions and collaborative teaching and learning in corporate workshops designed to enhance job satisfaction, interdependent teamwork, or occupational health and safety.

The life lessons and presentation format are relevant for participants of any educational level, from elementary school to college. The illustrations and the related discussion questions can be understood by anyone who can read, verbalize opinions, and answer questions. Of course, the teaching/learning success of a conversation about a life lesson will depend on the skill of a teacher or group facilitator at making the life-lesson discussions relevant for the particular participants.

The Language of Applied Behavioral Science (ABS)

Some language of psychologists is unique and quite different from that used in everyday discourse. Plus, behavioral scientists commonly use terminology that is uncommon in other domains of psychological science. Moreover, my students and I have coined certain AC4P terms, as well as distinct ways of defining some related psychological concepts. Thus, a *Glossary of Key Terms* used in this LifeCOACH manual is provided after Life Lesson 50, with definitions from an ***applied behavioral science*** (ABS) and an AC4P framework (i.e., ***humanistic behaviorism***).

Two terms in the preceding sentence are bold and italicized for an educational purpose. Specifically, a glossary term is bold and italicized in this text when it's used for the first time. This term might be italicized for emphasis later, as well as other words. Quotations are used to reflect words spoken by an individual or to call attention to unique or instructive language.

Even if you have had one or more courses in psychology, it could be useful to review the terms and definitions in the glossary. Many terms are defined with a behavioral and/or an AC4P focus, and this often results in a distinct difference from the more common usage of a term. For example, operational (i.e., behavioral or observable) definitions are offered whenever relevant and appropriate.

You might benefit from referring back to this *Glossary of Key Terms* when coming across particular ABS or AC4P jargon in the description of a life lesson. Plus, it's important to have a working definition of relevant key terms when discussing answers to questions designed to activate critical thinking, interpersonal conversation, and/or action planning relevant to a particular life lesson.

Responding to the Illustration

Directions: Look at the illustration above. Refer to this illustration to answer the following questions.

1. What does this illustration mean to you?
2. How might the environment (i.e., nurture) affect the student's report card?
3. How could heredity (i.e., nature) influence the student's report card?

LIFE LESSON 1

The Nature/Nurture Interaction

Decades ago this first life lesson was identified as the nature/nurture controversy. Today, the nature/nurture issue is no longer a question or a *controversy*. It's now understood that people's behavior results from an ongoing interaction between nature and nurture. Contemporary psychology—the science of human experience—addresses the impact of both personality traits (i.e., innate dispositions) and situational events (e.g., behavioral consequences) on human behaviors, attitudes, and emotions. For example, a primary mission of the burgeoning discipline of neuroscience is to identify connections between human behavior and specific areas and neuropathways of the brain. Identifying the behavioral functions of particular brain areas will presumably lead to improved interventions to benefit human welfare.

The significant impact of nature (e.g., biology and neurology) on behavior cannot be denied, but this LifeCOACH manual focuses on factors we can control for behavioral improvement. For example, two personality traits—conscientiousness and introversion—significantly influence people's behavior. When personality dispositions are treated like "states" rather than "traits," a nurture approach becomes relevant.

Regarding conscientiousness, situational factors can be established to increase an individual's *self-motivation*, persistence, and resilience, in spite of a relatively low score on a measure of conscientiousness. For those born with a proclivity to avoid human interaction (i.e., introverts), environmental conditions can be established to increase the occurrence of interpersonal communication for these folks. But of course, human interaction is more likely among extraverts, regardless of situational factors. And, this personality trait will interact with external factors to affect more interpersonal communication among extraverts than introverts.

Consider how a personality trait is analogous to handedness. While most of us were born with a preference to use our right or left hand (nature), we can teach ourselves to use the other hand quite well with instruction, practice, and behavioral feedback (nurture).

Thinking Beyond the Illustration

Directions: Based on what you have read for this life lesson, respond to the questions below.

1. How have you been influenced by the environment (i.e., nurture) to do good and/or bad?
2. How might your behavior be influenced by heredity (i.e., nature)? For example, do you have one or more personality traits that influence your actions? Please explain?

1

Responding to the Illustration

Directions: Look at the illustration above. Refer to this illustration to answer the following questions.

1. How does this illustration reflect this life lesson?
2. How much of what you do—your behavior—is influenced by an expectation of a positive or negative consequence?
3. What are some consequences (**rewards** or **penalties**) that influence your behavior these days?

LIFE LESSON 2

Behavior Is Motivated by Consequences

B.F. Skinner, the founder of the research and scholarship domain of experimental behavior analysis, is known for a simple but profound principle—*selection by consequences*.[1] Indeed, Skinner and his followers have demonstrated over and over that behavior occurs to gain positive *consequences* and to avoid or escape negative consequences. Plus, behavior can be modified by changing the events that follow it.

Influencing behavior by manipulating the environmental events that precede and follow a target behavior is called applied behavior analysis (ABA) by some and *applied behavioral science* (ABS) by others. ABA/ABS is the most successful approach for treating children with autism, and it has been applied worldwide to address the human dynamics of occupational health and safety (OH&S).

The application of behavioral science to prevent personal injuries and fatalities in the workplace is known as *behavior-based safety* (BBS) or behavioral safety in the corporate world.[2] Peer-to-peer coaching is a fundamental process of BBS. Workers develop a checklist of safe and at-risk behaviors and follow the steps of COACH as reviewed in the Preface—**C**are, **O**bserve, **A**nalyze, **C**ommunicate, and **H**elp.

At this point, it's most important to realize that much of our behavior is influenced by consequences we expect to gain, avoid, or escape by performing a particular behavior. We are motivated by behavioral consequences or the expected outcome(s) of our behavior. Realize also that the experimental and applied behavioral science (ABS) of analyzing and improving behavior is founded on this basic principle—behavior occurs to gain a positive consequence or to avoid or escape a negative consequence.

Other relevant life lessons in this LifeCOACH manual cover the following aspects of consequences which you might want to consider now: a) positive consequences are more effective than negative consequences at improving behavior, b) the best positive consequences activate and/or support self-motivation or self-directed behavior, and c) natural (or *intrinsic*) consequences have special advantages over extra (or *extrinsic*) consequences.

Thinking Beyond the Illustration

Directions: Based on what you have read for this life lesson, respond to the questions below.

1. What consequences (positive or negative) have been *unsuccessful* at influencing your behavior?
2. What behavior, if any, do you perform that is *not* motivated by an observable consequence?

Responding to the Illustration

Directions: Look at the illustration above. Refer to this illustration to answer the following questions.

1. What does the sign on the back of the vehicle mean to you?
2. Why might this sign work better to influence driving behavior than a simpler sign like "Please Drive Safely"?
3. Why is the girl (the driver) unhappy about the sign?

LIFE LESSON 3

Activate Behavior with Consequences

Applied behavioral science is founded on a basic **ABC** Model. "A" represents **activator** or the antecedent event(s) immediately preceding "B"—the behavior. "C" stands for the *consequence*—event(s) following a behavior that influence its recurrence.

An activator is an **incentive** when it announces the availability of a positive consequence—a *reward*—following the occurrence of a particular desirable behavior. In contrast, an activator is a **disincentive** when it announces the availability of a negative consequence—a *penalty*—following the occurrence of a designated undesirable behavior.

In this illustration, the sign—an activator—could be an incentive or a disincentive, depending on the perception of the driver. In this case, the driver sees the sign as a disincentive because she expects other drivers to report only occurrences of the undesirable or unsafe driving behaviors they observe.

Why doesn't the driver expect a phone call about desirable (i.e., safe) driving behavior? Is this because the driver will not be driving safely and not be eligible for a positive phone call? Of course not, but it would be instructive to discuss various answers to this question.

You will likely come to the disappointing conclusion that people are more likely to notice and criticize undesirable behavior than notice and recognize desirable behavior. This is a critical issue and the theme of Life Lesson 8.

Consider how our culture influences a focus on undesirable behavior, and the use of negative consequences to eliminate such behavior. The news media reports more about unwanted than wanted behavior, and the government approach to behavioral control is to pass a law and enforce it. We seem to live in a "Click It or Ticket" society.

But as explained in Life Lesson 2, behavioral science has demonstrated various advantages of using positive over negative consequences to increase the frequency and/or improve the quality of behavior.

Thinking Beyond the Illustration

Directions: Based on what you have read for this life lesson, respond to the questions below.

1. What kind of driving behaviors (safe or unsafe) would be reported more often? Why?
2. What signs or messages in your current life space might be more powerful if they included a consequence?

Responding to the Illustration

Directions: Look at the illustration above. Refer to this illustration to answer the following questions.

1. What will happen to the money under the sign if the waitress shows an improvement in her service?
2. What will happen to the pile of bills under the sign if the waitress shows a decrease in her service?
3. Do you think this technique would influence the behavior of the server(s) where you dine out? Why or why not?

LIFE LESSON 4

Manage Behavior with Extrinsic Consequences

The illustration for this life lesson depicts a fundamental intervention for changing behavior, as illustrated and discussed for Life Lesson 3. The table sign provides both an incentive and a disincentive. This activator indicates that more money (i.e., a reward) will be added following desirable service behavior of the waitress, but money will be taken away (i.e., a penalty) if the service of the waitress is below expectations. Incentives and disincentives are considered *if-then contingencies*. If you perform a certain behavior you will receive a positive consequence (an incentive/reward contingency) or a negative consequence (a disincentive/penalty contingency). Managing behavior with an incentive/reward contingency and/or a disincentive/penalty contingency is termed *contingency management*.

An *if-then contingency* could be stated as an opportunity to perform an enjoyable activity (e.g., watch a favorite T.V. show) after performing a less pleasant but desirable behavior (e.g., complete a certain work assignment). This contingency is based on the finding that behaviors occurring naturally at high rates can be used to increase the occurrence of behaviors occurring at low rates.[3] Students use this *management* technique when they reward themselves with a desirable behavior (e.g., read and send a text message) after completing a certain class assignment.

Parents who reward their children for desirable behaviors (e.g., making their bed, reading a book, or practicing a musical instrument) or for desirable outcomes of behavior (e.g., high grades in school, a book report, or a clean bedroom) are motivating desirable behavior with *contingency management*.

Most salary employees and wage-workers receive a regular paycheck after a certain time (e.g., after one or two weeks). However, since this financial compensation is usually not determined by the occurrence of designated behaviors, most employers and supervisors are not benefiting from contingency management.

Thinking Beyond the Illustration

Directions: Based on what you have read for this life lesson, respond to the questions below.

1. How does the table sign in the illustration reflect the power of behavioral consequences (i.e., Life Lesson 2)?
2. What other signs like this could be used to influence behavior in your life space? Please explain.

7

Responding to the Illustration

Directions: Look at the illustration above. Refer to this illustration to answer the following questions.

1. Why did Billy complete the math problem?
2. What might happen if Billy does not receive an extrinsic reward for his problem-solving behavior?
3. What is a natural or intrinsic positive consequence for Billy's correct response? How could the teacher help Billy appreciate that intrinsic consequence?

LIFE LESSON 5

Promote Natural Positive Consequences

The illustration for this life lesson reveals a criticism that various pop-psychology books have used to discredit the use of positive consequences or rewards to increase the frequency of desirable behavior. This critique is reflected by the title of one of those books: *Punished by Rewards: The Trouble with Gold Stars, Incentive Plans, A's, Praise, and Other Bribes*.[4] Authored by a journalist and published in 1993, this popular self-help book caused quite a stir among behavioral scientists who have researched and demonstrated the benefits of using positive consequences to motivate behavior since the 1950s.

Systematic reviews of research related to the pop-psychology critique of *extrinsic* rewards have revealed the following: a) As illustrated in Life Lessons 2, 3, and 4, consequences desired by participants increase the frequency of the targeted behavior, and b) When behavioral rewards are removed, the target behavior decreases in frequency of occurrence, as your common sense indicates. However, there is limited evidence that the target behavior occurs less often than its pre-reward or baseline frequency, as is assumed by the uninformed authors of books that demean the use of behavioral rewards.[5]

Here is the most practical conclusion from relevant behavioral-science research of extrinsic rewards: When extrinsic rewards are used to get a desirable behavior started, those positive consequences should be *faded* (i.e., given intermittently after the target behavior), and natural or *intrinsic* consequences should be emphasized, such as the meaningfulness or the longer-term purpose of the target behavior.

The natural consequences of a target behavior should be identified at the start of a motivational process, but it often takes an extrinsic consequence to motivate initial participation and enable recognition of the natural longer-term benefits of the behavior.

Consider how airlines, hotels, banks, and grocery stores motivate customers with coupons or "reward points." With natural consequences unavailable to influence consumer choice, patrons often endure inconvenience or less comfort to earn those extrinsic rewards.

Thinking Beyond the Illustration

Directions: Based on what you have read for this life lesson, respond to the questions below.

1. To what extent does the extrinsic consequence of a grade on a test motivate you to study and/or attend class?
2. What intrinsic consequences do you experience from studying course material and/or attending class? Please explain.

Responding to the Illustration

Directions: Look at the illustration above. Refer to this illustration to answer the following questions.

1. How do Dad, Mom, and their son feel about their backyard chores?
2. Are the family members working to achieve positive consequences or avoid negative consequences?
3. What are the various consequences motivating the behavior of Mom, Dad, and their son?

LIFE LESSON 6

The Power of Natural Consequences

The motivating consequences discussed in Life Lessons 2, 3, and 4 are considered extra or *extrinsic stimuli* added to a situation to motivate behavior. For example, children might clean up their room for an extra dessert at dinner; students study for an exam to achieve a passing grade; and factory workers do their jobs for wages. This life lesson addresses the natural consequences that follow behavior and keep it going.

Some of these natural (or *intrinsic*) consequences are immediate while others are delayed. In the illustration, each person is experiencing immediate natural consequences—the fruits of their labor. But Dad and Mom are likely anticipating a delayed consequence, such as a large shade tree and a garden that provides vegetables. While their son is experiencing an immediate intrinsic consequence or a positive **reinforcer** for his car-washing behavior, he might be thinking of later impressing a date with a clean car.

Are you thinking that intrinsic or natural consequences are more powerful than extrinsic or extra consequences? Yes, your common sense is right because you've been there. You've experienced the flow of behavior that is motivated by immediate natural consequences, including, for example, entertainment from reading and watching T.V. or the sense of accomplishment from playing a musical instrument, exercising, cooking, or applying artistic skills to drawing, painting, or wood-working.

What about pushing those buttons on your computer, iPad, or cell phone? Some call this an addiction and the cause of distracted driving and even distracted walking. This life lesson reveals the truth. Such behavior is not a disease; instead, it is the outcome of devices that reinforce the flow of behavior with soon, certain, positive, and intrinsic consequences.

Besides texting while driving and walking, many other undesirable behaviors are supported by natural, soon, certain, and positive consequences or *intrinsic positive reinforcers* (e.g., excessive alcohol consumption, cigarette and marijuana smoking, and over-eating).

Thinking Beyond the Illustration

Directions: Based on what you have read for this life lesson, respond to the questions below.

1. What behaviors do you perform regularly that are not motivated by an extra or extrinsic consequence like money, praise, or a grade?
2. What natural or intrinsic consequences motivate you to perform those behaviors? Please explain.

Responding to the Illustration

Directions: Look at the illustration above. Refer to this illustration to answer the following questions.

1. What life lesson is reflected in this illustration?
2. Why would humans perform better at culinary school than dogs?
3. When is it desirable to resist a soon, certain, and positive consequence for one that is delayed, uncertain, and positive?

LIFE LESSON 7

The Power of Emotional Intelligence

Have you ever heard a statement such as, "Your success in life depends upon your ability to delay immediate pleasures for future longer-term accomplishment"? In fact, research suggests that one's ability to keep working in the face of temptation to engage in an activity with more immediate positive consequences reflects *emotional intelligence* (EQ), and EQ is quite predictive of career success.[6]

To verify the direct relationship between ability to delay immediate gratification and future success, Walter Mischel gave four-year-olds a "Marshmallow Test" to measure their impulse control.[7] He handed children a marshmallow and said they could eat it now or wait until later and receive two marshmallows. Some children ate the single marshmallow within a few seconds after the researcher left the room. The other children were able to wait the 15 to 20 minutes for the researcher to return.

Most children who delayed their immediate gratification for a delayed but larger reward did not just sit patiently and wait. Instead, they engaged in behaviors that apparently facilitated their self-discipline to resist the impulse for immediate pleasure. Some sang or talked to themselves; others played games with their hands and feet; and others covered their eyes or buried their head in their arms.

When these adolescents were evaluated 14 years later during their last year of high school, those who had waited patiently at four were far superior as students than were those who had failed the Marshmallow Test. They were more academically competent; they had better study habits; and they appeared to be more eager to learn. They were better able to concentrate, to express their ideas, and to set goals and achieve them.

In fact, these higher achievers scored significantly higher on both the math and verbal portions of the scholastic achievement test (SAT)—by an average of 210 total points—than did the students who had not delayed gratification at age four.[8] While it's tempting to consider EQ as a fact of nature, research indicates EQ can be learned and nurtured by applying the life lessons in this manual (e.g., Life Lessons 17–20).[6]

Thinking Beyond the Illustration

Directions: Based on what you have read for this life lesson, respond to the questions below.

1. When have you regretted going for an immediate positive consequence instead of waiting for a larger but delayed positive consequence?
2. What technique(s) have you used to control the temptation to go for immediate pleasures and work for larger but delayed positive consequences?

Responding to the Illustration

Directions: Look at the illustration above. Refer to this illustration to answer the following questions.

1. What do you think the coach said to the player?
2. Praising a player for good behavior is called **supportive feedback**, whereas pointing out a player's bad behavior is **corrective feedback**. What kind of **feedback** is shown here?
3. How did the player feel after getting the coach's feedback?

LIFE LESSON 8

Use More Supportive Feedback

We learn more from our mistakes." How many times have you heard something like that? While this might allow us to feel better about the errors of our ways and provide an excuse for focusing more on people's failures than on their successes, nothing could be further from the truth. Behavioral scientists have shown convincingly that success—not failure—produces the most effective learning.[9]

Recognition following a desirable behavior is termed *supportive feedback*; negative commentary after a mistake is considered *corrective feedback*. In both cases, the desirable or undesirable behavior should be specified and behavior-focused feedback should be offered. However, it's critical to be *directive* when offering supportive recognition but *nondirective* when offering correction.

When delivering supportive feedback you should indicate directly what behavior you noticed that is appreciated. However, with corrective feedback it's best to ask questions first. The objective is to get the feedback recipient to accept your observation of less-than-optimal behavior and then state a sincere intention to improve. This is more likely to happen if you (the observer) do *not* begin the corrective-feedback conversation by specifying the behavior needing correction followed by directions for behavior change.

Corrective feedback should begin with questions designed to learn the perspective of the person observed with regard to the behavior needing improvement, as well as the relevant circumstances. Listen attentively to explanations or excuses for performing the undesirable behavior. This could uncover environmental or system factors that motivated or facilitated performance of the unwanted behavior and/or inhibited an occurrence of a desirable alternative.

I hope it's obvious that the overly popular term "constructive criticism" is an oxymoron—contradictory words. For most people, criticism reflects something negative about a person's attitude, character, or personality. Only with a focus on behavior can correction be accepted and constructive.

Thinking Beyond the Illustration

Directions: Based on what you have read for this life lesson, respond to the questions below.

1. What effect could public criticism from a coach to an athlete have on other members of a team?
2. Have you ever been in a situation like the soccer player in the illustration? Please describe your behavior, the feedback you received, and your feelings.

Responding to the Illustration

Directions: Look at the illustration above. Refer to this illustration to answer the following questions.

1. What is the message of the illustration above?
2. Do you believe people receive less praise or recognition than criticism or correction?
3. Why do people provide more correction for undesirable behavior than support for desirable behavior?

LIFE LESSON 9

The Power of Behavioral Praise

Words of approval, appreciation, and praise for commendable behavior are relatively rare, especially when compared to the use of verbal reprimands or correction for undesirable behavior. As discussed in Life Lesson 8, learning is more effective and enjoyable when success is rewarded more often than errors are penalized.

Mistakes or disruptive behaviors stick out and invite attention and corrective action (Life Lesson 3); desirable behavior, on the other hand, does not naturally attract attention and seemingly does not require intervention such as behavioral recognition, praise, or statements of gratitude.

Both research and common sense tell us it's extremely beneficial to call attention to behaviors we want to see occur more often and to recognize those desirable behaviors appropriately. Behavioral scientists refer to these positive consequences as **now-that rewards** as opposed to *if-then rewards*. An *if-then* reward reflects an incentive, as discussed in Life Lesson 4. "If you do this desired behavior, then I will give you this reward."

A *now-that* reward is different. There is no incentive, just a *reward* or a sincere statement of appreciation for the desirable behavior you observed. The delivery of *now-that* recognition is simple and straightforward. You specify the desirable behavior and offer sincere praise, recognition, and/or gratitude.

The result: You might increase occurrences of the recognized behavior, and you will surely enhance the person's perception of personal competence and self-motivation (as discussed later in Life Lesson 18).

As introduced by Dale Carnegie in his classic best seller, *How to Win Friends and Influence People,* everyone wants to feel important.[10] Behavioral praise not only enhances **self-esteem**, it fuels a perception of competence at performing certain desirable behaviors. Psychologists call this **self-efficacy,** [11] and this **person-state** is key to being self-motivated (Life Lesson 18) and feeling empowered (Life Lesson 25).

Thinking Beyond the Illustration

Directions: Based on what you have read for this life lesson, respond to the questions below.

1. When was the last time you thanked a family member for something s/he did for you? Please describe the circumstance.
2. Why is it important to give and receive gratitude for kind and thoughtful behavior? (We call such behavior **actively caring for people—AC4P**.)

Responding to the Illustration

Directions: Look at the illustration above. Refer to this illustration to answer the following questions.

1. Will the runner in this illustration take off running fast? Why?
2. How will the runner feel about the coach who motivates his behavior with the approach shown in the illustration?
3. Will the athlete continue running when the coach is not around to hold him accountable?

Promote Success Seeking

T he most efficient and effective way to improve both behavior and attitude at the same time is to follow a desirable behavior with a positive consequence—from a material reward to personal recognition or praise (Life Lesson 9).

In fact, people usually have a positive mindset or disposition when they are working to earn a positive consequence, as when students work on a homework assignment to achieve a high grade or words of approval from their teacher. In these situations, participants are considered *success seekers*—their behavior is motivated by expectations of a pleasant consequence or outcome.[12]

Sometimes behavior occurs to avoid or escape a negative or aversive consequence. These are the drivers who buckle up and comply with the speed limit to avoid a traffic ticket; and they are the students who study for a test to avoid a failing grade or complete a homework assignment to avoid a reprimand from their teacher. These individuals are termed *failure avoiders*.[13]

As your common sense reveals, *success seekers* are happier and more optimistic than *failure avoiders*, and they accomplish more. Compared to failure avoiding, when students are success seekers they have a more positive attitude toward their classes and they feel more empowered and in control of their grades. Please note: The same situation can be interpreted as success seeking or failure avoiding. Is the student motivated to achieve success (e.g., increased knowledge or a good grade) or to avoid failure (e.g., a poor grade)? The success-seeking student says, "I *get* to go to class; it's an *opportunity*." The failure-avoiding student says, "I've *got* to go to class; it's a *requirement*."

We're talking about a mindset that is activated and supported by interpersonal and intrapersonal conversation, as covered later in Life Lessons 18 and 38, respectively. A focus on loss control in the business world can fuel a mindset of failure avoiding over success seeking.

Thinking Beyond the Illustration

Directions: Based on what you have read for this life lesson, respond to the questions below.

1. Is there a better—more positive—way to motivate behavior than that shown in the illustration? Please explain.
2. Describe a behavior you perform to avoid a negative consequence and a behavior you perform to achieve a positive consequence. For which behavior is your attitude more positive?

Responding to the Illustration

Directions: Look at the illustration above. Refer to this illustration to answer the following questions.

1. How is the student in the illustration feeling?
2. Will the comment from Dad make his daughter feel better? Why or why not?
3. Is the comment from Dad useful in providing behavioral direction or achievement motivation?

LIFE LESSON 11

Make Feedback Behavioral

As discussed in Life Lessons 8, 9, and 10, supportive feedback is a powerful way to enhance a learning process and help a person feel competent. However, to provide optimal direction and support, supportive feedback needs to be associated directly with the desired behavior. When people know what they did to earn sincere appreciation or praise, they are more likely to be motivated to perform that behavior again.

If it's necessary to delay the supportive feedback, the conversation should relive the activity deserving positive recognition. Talk specifically about the behavior that warrants special acknowledgment. If possible, ask the recipient to recall aspects of the situation and the commendable behavior.

The illustration for this life lesson actually calls for corrective feedback. For corrective feedback to be effective, the behavior in need of correction needs to be identified. But as suggested in Life Lesson 8, a **nondirective stance** is recommended. Questions are asked initially to gain an understanding of the situation from the perspective of the person needing corrective feedback. In the case of the undesirable report card (i.e., undesirable *performance*), Dad should ask his daughter to identify the behaviors that led to the low grades, and then to specify what behaviors could improve the next report card.

Dad should listen actively to his daughter's explanations or excuses for the low grades, and then ask her what she will do to improve her grades. Dad's objective is to obtain some ownership of the poor outcome, including the excuses, along with a personal intention to improve.

Dad should help his daughter list specific behaviors needed to improve her grades. As discussed in Life Lesson 9, strategic applications of *if-then* rewards might be called for. Of course, both parents should periodically deliver sincere *now-that* praise when they observe their daughter performing behavior related to grade improvement. The next life lesson explains how to give praise effectively.

Thinking Beyond the Illustration

Directions: Based on what you have read for this life lesson, respond to the questions below.

1. What kind of communication from Dad in the illustration could be more useful?
2. What kind of support from the student's parents could improve the grades on their daughter's next report card?

Responding to the Illustration

Directions: Look at the illustration above. Refer to this illustration to answer the following questions.

1. What does the illustration mean to you?
2. Does Mom appreciate the praise from her daughter? Why or why not?
3. Recall a time when you received praise for something you did well. Who gave you that praise and how did it make you feel?

LIFE LESSON 12

Make Praise Genuine

Sometimes people are suspicious of the genuineness of praise when it's delivered face to face. Is there an ulterior motive? Perhaps a favor is expected in return, as depicted in the illustration for this life lesson. Consider the following guidelines for giving quality praise—a *now-that* verbal reward (Life Lesson 9).

Be behavioral. Refer to the specific behavior that warrants the recognition. When people know what they did to earn the praise, they are apt to perform that behavior again.

Make it personal. When you recognize someone, you're expressing personal thanks for the behavior you saw. You should customize your words to fit a particular person and the circumstances.

Take it to a higher level. After identifying the praiseworthy behavior, add a positive characteristic like *leadership*, integrity, trustworthiness, or *actively caring* to make the supportive feedback more meaningful, memorable, and rewarding. "Johnny, the support you gave your sister on her homework shows your talent as an actively caring mentor and leader."

Deliver it privately. The popular slogan, "Praise publicly and reprimand privately" is wrong. Recognition should be personal, private, and one-to-one. In fact, some individuals feel embarrassed when singled out in front of their peers. They might even fear harassment from those who did not get the praise.

Let it sink in. Resist any temptation to cover other issues after giving behavioral praise. By keeping your positive words most salient you allow your recognition to stand alone and sink in. This optimizes the possibility of positive self-talk by the praise recipient and can fuel his or her self-motivation to continue the exemplary behavior.

Second-hand recognition occurs when you relay a positive comment you heard from someone about the recipient's behavior. Such indirect praise can actually feel most genuine and nurture a sense of belongingness and interdependency (Life Lessons 19 & 20).

Thinking Beyond the Illustration

Directions: Based on what you have read for this life lesson, respond to the questions below.

1. Recall the last time you gave someone praise or recognition for his or her behavior. What was the behavior you recognized and how did giving such behavioral praise make you feel?
2. Do you deserve more praise or recognition for your commendable behavior than you receive? Please explain.

23

Responding to the Illustration

Directions: Look at the illustration above. Refer to this illustration to answer the following questions.

1. What does this illustration mean to you?
2. Did Mom realize she was teaching her daughter to drive fast?
3. When are people most likely to observe the behavior of others and learn as a result?

LIFE LESSON 13

The Power of Observational Learning

I f you want to be better at what you do, watch someone who performs that behavior better than you. The power of *observational learning* is obvious, right? Your actions are the result of observational learning whenever you do something in a particular way—you saw someone else do it that way, or someone showed you how to do it that way, or characters on television or in a video game did it that way.

Children learn numerous behavioral patterns by watching their parents, teachers, and peers. When they see their siblings or schoolmates receive positive recognition for certain behaviors, they are more likely to copy that behavior. This process is termed *vicarious reinforcement*.[14] At the same time, when children observe others receive a negative consequence for performing certain behaviors, they learn to avoid or stop those behaviors. This is referred to as *vicarious punishment*.[14]

Whenever parents remind their children to set an example, they are alluding to the critical influence of observational learning. Consider the beneficial example(s) you set when you practice the life lessons revealed in this LifeCOACH manual.

At this point the life lessons have prescribed a) how to give behavior-based supportive feedback; b) how to take a nondirective stance when giving behavior-based corrective feedback; and c) the need to give frequent and genuine positive "now-that" recognition, appreciation, and/or gratitude for desirable behavior you observe. More interpersonal coaching needs to follow those recommendations for initiating and supporting continuous improvement. When you practice these behaviors, at least one other person (i.e., the recipient of your feedback) learns desirable coaching behavior through observation.

Now consider the potential observational learning resulting from *second-hand recognition*. When you tell people the positive commentary you heard from another person about their performance, you set the example for spreading positive over negative gossip and you contribute to cultivating an *AC4P culture*.

Thinking Beyond the Illustration

Directions: Based on what you have read for this life lesson, respond to the questions below.

1. What desirable and undesirable behaviors have you learned by watching the behavior of other people?
2. How might your behavior—past, present, or future—influence the behavior of others?

Responding to the Illustration

Directions: Look at the illustration above. Refer to this illustration to answer the following questions.

1. What does this illustration mean to you?
2. Does television show more desirable or undesirable behavior? Please offer some examples of each.
3. What have you learned by watching television?

LIFE LESSON 14

Behavioral Observations Teach Social Acceptance

Life Lesson 13 focused on learning from watching others. This related life lesson targets the social influence of behavioral observations. In this case, the observer is not learning a new behavior, but learns what behavior is acceptable or unacceptable in certain situations. We are particularly observant of the behaviors of others when we're in an unfamiliar setting. We watch what others are doing and saying in order to fit in.

We're talking about the power of the social influence *Principle of Conformity*, or *social proof* as labeled by Robert Cialdini.[15] Do you choose what clothes to wear at a social event by observing the attire of others, or at least by anticipating what others will wear? For example, before an event you might ask a friend what attire is appropriate.

Have you ever selected a restaurant by noting the number of cars in the parking lot? *Social proof*: The more cars, the better the food. Today, Internet rating services and personal testimonies indicate social acceptance and have considerable influence over concomitant behavior.

How many males have stopped shaving regularly after observing the facial hair of other males? Have you modified your verbal behavior in a particular context after noting what others were saying? Have you modified the frequency of certain teaching or parenting styles after observing the behavior of other teachers or parents? Has your vehicle driving changed as a result of what you see other drivers doing (e.g., texting, speeding, signaling turns, waving a sign of gratitude)?

This list of behaviors influenced by observing others could go on and on, but I'm sure you get the point. While we might not learn new behaviors by observing others, we learn where and when certain learned behaviors should be performed or inhibited. But consider this: We usually don't want to admit we are practicing a certain behavior because we saw someone else do it, right? People like to believe their behavior is their idea—not influenced by the behavior of someone else. We are influenced by the *Principle of Conformity*, but we don't like to admit it.

Thinking Beyond the Illustration

Directions: Based on what you have read for this life lesson, respond to the questions below.

1. How does television influence the occurrence of behavior you have already learned?
2. Do you think people in general have become more aggressive or violent as a result of T.V. watching? Why or why not?

Responding to the Illustration

Directions: Look at the illustration above. Refer to this illustration to answer the following questions.

1. Does this illustration reflect observational learning (Life Lesson 13), conformity (Life Lesson 14), or both? Please explain.
2. Is the behavior requested of Ethel in the illustration desirable? Please explain why or why not?
3. Why is Ethel trying so hard to match the rocking behavior of the other "rockers"?

LIFE LESSON 15

Social Norms Are Injunctive and/or Descriptive

As reviewed in Life Lesson 13, *observational learning* simply means we learn by watching other people and we teach others by our own examples. Sometimes the example set by others does not teach us a new behavior, but instead it informs us that a behavior we know how to perform is appropriate or desirable at a particular time and place. We conform to gain approval from others and/or to avoid disapproval from others.

People also gain information by observing the behavior of others. This is considered normative influence or *social proof* (Life Lesson 14) and defines a social norm. Social norms are injunctive or descriptive. An ***injunctive norm*** defines desirable behavior, or what people "ought to do."[15] In the United States, for example, walking on the right side of stairs is an injunctive norm. And vehicle drivers would experience strong disapproval via shouting, horn honking, and perhaps some negative hand gesturing if they were observed driving on the left side of the road. This is not the case in England or Australia, of course.

A ***descriptive norm*** is the common and observed behavior of other people. Are people hiking, running, or biking on a trail? A credible person performing a certain behavior can alter one's perception of the descriptive norm. One person littering can prompt onlookers to litter. Of course, the same is possible if a credible person picks up litter. In this case, picking up litter is obviously an injunctive norm.

Injunctive norms are not necessarily descriptive and, as depicted in the illustration for this life lesson, descriptive norms are not necessarily injunctive. But behavior reflecting an injunctive norm can be activated by a descriptive norm. For example, guests at a hotel were most likely to re-use their towels to conserve energy when the message that requested them to hang up their used towels for re-use included the descriptive message that the prior guests who had stayed in their room re-used their towels.[17]

As revealed in Life Lesson 14, people "go along to get along" and to "fit in"; however, we generally don't like to feel influenced or controlled by others. The next life lesson builds on this premise.

Thinking Beyond the Illustration

Directions: Based on what you have read for this life lesson, respond to the questions below.

1. What desirable and undesirable behaviors have you seen that were influenced by conformity?
2. Have you been influenced to do something just because you heard others were doing it? Please explain and indicate whether the behavior was appropriate, inappropriate, or neither.

Responding to the Illustration

Directions: Look at the illustration above. Refer to this illustration to answer the following questions.

1. What is the boy in the illustration trying to prove?
2. What kind of sign could reduce the occurrence of this contrary behavior?
3. Have you ever felt like disregarding a top-down rule or mandate? When did that happen and why did you feel that way?

LIFE LESSON 16

Mandates Can Activate Contrary Behavior

Everyone likes to experience a perception of *choice* or autonomy. Much research in psychological science has shown that individuals of all ages are more likely to be self-motivated and self-directed when they perceive some degree of *personal control* or choice. When people believe they have some degree of personal choice in a particular situation, they need less *extrinsic* accountability from others to keep them motivated.[18]

In contrast, top-down threats of negative consequences for undesirable behavior not only decrease a person's perception of personal choice and self-motivation, they can actually motivate occurrences of the undesired behavior in situations where they cannot be observed. Why? Because behavior contrary to a mandate enables a regaining of personal choice or freedom. This is especially the case in cultures where individualism or independence is a priority, as it is in the United States.

Yes, individuals usually comply with rules or mandates when they can be observed and held accountable for their transgressions. But what do they do when performing alone? For example, in one field study, college students whose parents had threatened harsh penalties if they were caught consuming alcohol drank the most number of alcoholic beverages when away from home, and they got the most intoxicated.[19]

In schools, students are often viewed as passive learners, because teachers plan, execute, and evaluate most aspects of the teaching/learning process. In this case, students' perceptions of personal choice are limited—along with their self-motivation, perhaps.

However, cooperative teaching/learning situations in which students contribute to the selection and presentation of course material is most beneficial, especially over the long term.[20]

In the workplace, employees are more supportive of and engaged in work programs or processes they helped to create.[21] One explanation for these findings is that the perception of personal choice fuels self-motivation, as explained further in our next life lesson.

Thinking Beyond the Illustration

Directions: Based on what you have read for this life lesson, respond to the questions below.

1. Have you ever actually disregarded a rule or regulation? If yes, please describe the details of the circumstances for one such event.
2. What could parents, teachers, coaches, or work supervisors do to influence people to be more likely to follow their rules or instructions?

Responding to the Illustration

Directions: Look at the illustration above. Refer to this illustration to answer the following questions.

1. Who has the perception of choice in the illustration? Why?
2. How does the illustration show that choice is a personal belief or perception?
3. Explain how this illustration reflects the phrase, "Choice is in the eyes of the beholder."

LIFE LESSON 17

The Power of Perceived Choice

At times, people need external activators (e.g., incentives) and consequences (e.g., rewards) to keep them motivated (Life Lessons 2, 3, & 4). Psychologists call these *extrinsic motivators* and teachers use these to keep students on track (e.g., grades on assignments and tests). But sometimes people develop *self-motivation* and *self-accountability* within the context of an extrinsic accountability system.

Sometimes students study and participate in learning activities for personal or internal consequences. They perform for more than a grade. Researchers have defined conditions that facilitate such *self-directed behavior* and *self-motivation*. In particular, conditions that increase a person's perception of choice or personal control enhance that individual's self-motivation.

Please note we're talking about the perception of choice, as reflected in the illustration for this life lesson. You've certainly experienced the pleasure of having alternatives to choose from, and feeling in control of those factors is critical for successful self-directed performance. How sweet the taste of success when we can attribute our achievement to our own choices.

Imagine helping a young boy dress in nice clothes you have selected for him to wear on his first day of school. This could feel like top-down control to the boy, and he might resist in order to assert his individuality or personal freedom (Life Lesson 16).

Now consider an alternative approach: Select two school outfits you would like the boy to wear, and let him choose between the two. More than likely, the young boy will be less resistant because he feels he has some choice in the clothes he will wear to school.

Self-motivation is also fueled by the perception of being competent at performing worthwhile work. Note the connection to feeling important,[10] as discussed in Life Lesson 9. The next life lesson explains how to make that happen. Then Life Lesson 19 explains the third determinant of self-motivation—a spirit of win/win *interdependence*.

Thinking Beyond the Illustration

Directions: Based on what you have read for this life lesson, respond to the questions below.

1. Describe two situations (past or present)—one in which you felt/feel no choice and one in which you felt/feel some choice.
2. How might a situation in which you currently perceive no choice be changed to allow some feelings of personal choice?

Responding to the Illustration

Directions: Look at the illustration above. Refer to this illustration to answer the following questions.

1. What does this illustration mean to you?
2. What does it mean to say someone has a "big head"?
3. Have you ever felt that you received too many compliments for your good work or desirable behavior? Please explain your answer.

LIFE LESSON 18

The Power of Building Competence

"People are not successful because they are motivated; they are motivated because they are successful."[22] This provocative quotation reflects the powerful role of perceived *competence* in motivating people to continue working diligently on a task when no one is watching them or holding them accountable.

Much research has shown that people become more self-motivated and self-directed when they feel competent at performing worthwhile work.[21] Offering genuine praise, recognition, or supportive feedback can make that happen. Please recall Life Lessons 8 and 9, and consider your related discussions on delivering supportive behavioral feedback.

Just the language we use when talking to ourselves (self-talk) and to others (interpersonal) can impact perceptions of personal choice and competence. For example, which of the following nine pairs of words or phrases connect more to a perception of choice and/or competence and hence to self-motivation?

"occupant restraint" or "vehicle safety belt"?
"requirement" or "opportunity"?
"peer pressure" or "peer support"?
"training" or "mentoring"?
"mandate" or "expectation"?
"compliance" or "accomplishment"?
"I've got to do this" or "I get to do this"?
"I must meet this deadline" or "I choose to achieve another milestone"?
"I awaken to an alarm clock" or "I awaken to my opportunity clock"?

I'm sure you see how the language on the right relates more to a perception of choice, personal control, and/or competence and can influence self-motivation. The next life lesson reveals more we can do to activate and support self-motivation in ourselves and others.

Thinking Beyond the Illustration

Directions: Based on what you have read for this life lesson, respond to the questions below.

1. Have you ever felt that you deserved a compliment but did not receive it? If yes, please explain one of those situations.
2. In general, do you believe more compliments should be delivered for commendable behavior? Why or why not?

Responding to the Illustration

Directions: Look at the illustration above. Refer to this illustration to answer the following questions.

1. What does the term **_independent_** mean to you?
2. If independent means "doing it yourself," what does the term interdependent mean?
3. What kinds of situations or circumstances reflect interdependence?

LIFE LESSON 19

The Power of Interdependence

E d Deci and Richard Flaste affirm we have three basic psychological needs, and when these needs are satisfied, we are self-motivated.[23] Specifically, self-motivation is activated by conditions that facilitate fulfillment of our needs for autonomy (or choice), competence, and relatedness (or interdependence).

We addressed the connection between choice and self-motivation in Life Lesson 17, and between competence and self-motivation in Life Lesson 18. Now, let's consider the power of an *interdependent* rather than an *independent* mindset.

An interdependent spirit reflects systems thinking or relatedness beyond the confines of family, social groups, and work teams. In other words, *interdependence* represents an *actively-caring-for-people (AC4P)* mindset for humankind in general—a relatedness or interconnectedness with others that transcends political differences and prejudices, and profoundly respects and appreciates diversity. Developing a relatedness or interdependent spirit in an organization, a classroom, or a family unit leads to two primary human-performance payoffs: a) individuals become more self-motivated to do the right thing, and b) people are more likely to actively care for the well-being of others.

With this life lesson, we have covered the three evidence-based person-states that determine whether an individual is self-motivated: a) autonomy or perceived choice (Life Lesson 17), b) perceived competence (Life Lesson 18), and c) interdependence (Life Lesson 19). Dispositional, interpersonal, and environmental conditions that enhance these three person-states augment one's self-motivation and increase occurrences of self-directed and discretionary behavior.

Proper applications of the life lessons covered so far and explained further in Life Lessons 20 and 21 can increase perceptions of one or more of the person-states that fuel self-motivation and self-directed behavior.

Thinking Beyond the Illustration

Directions: Based on what you have read for this life lesson, respond to the questions below.

1. When might it be better to have a mindset or perspective for interdependence rather than independence?
2. Are there times when independence is more appropriate than interdependence? Please explain.

Responding to the Illustration

Directions: Look at the illustration above. Refer to this illustration to answer the following questions.

1. What does the illustration mean to you?
2. How is a win/lose perspective or mindset different from a win/win perspective or mindset?
3. What situations or circumstances reflect a win/lose perspective or mindset?

LIFE LESSON 20

The Power of a Win/Win Mindset

Consider these popular slogans in American culture: "Nice guys finish last," "You've got to blow your own horn," and "The squeaky wheel gets the grease." Now consider these quotations, popular in Japan: "One does not make the wind, but is blown by it," and "The nail that rises above the board invites a hammering down."

These quotations reflect an *independent (individualistic)* or an *interdependent (collectivistic)* mindset or perspective. Although team sports make a win/lose viewpoint quite prominent to observers (especially fans), the members of a sports team benefit from an interdependent or collectivistic mindset.

As reflected by another quotation, "There's no I in team," and an acronym for TEAM (Together Everyone Achieves More), the performance of a team gains more from interdependent than independent behavior. Of course, this life lesson connects directly to Life Lesson 19 on the power of interdependence and self-motivation.

We come into this world dependent on others to take care of us. Children depend on parents or caregivers for all their basic needs. In contrast, adolescents look for opportunities to be on their own. In fact, it seems a primary mission of most teenagers is to resist dependency and become independent.

This reliance on self (independence) rather than others (interdependence) is promoted and supported throughout U.S. culture, from high-school and college classrooms to corporate boardrooms. But high-performance teamwork actually requires a *reciprocal dependency*—team members depending on each other to complete their task assignments. This reflects a shift from independence to interdependence and a sense of **community**.

With an interdependent community spirit, we trust others to do their part for the organization; and with self-motivation, we choose to contribute our competence for the benefit of others in our group or team.

Thinking Beyond the Illustration

Directions: Based on what you have read for this life lesson, respond to the questions below.

1. What situations or circumstances have you experienced or observed that reflect a win/win perspective?
2. What are the benefits of a win/win over a win/lose perspective or mindset?

Responding to the Illustration

Directions: Look at the illustration above. Refer to this illustration to answer the following questions.

1. With the donkey representing the Democratic political party and the elephant standing for Republicans, what does the illustration mean to you?
2. Can you connect Life Lesson 20 on the power of a win/win perspective with this illustration?
3. How might a group of individuals shift from a win/lose perspective to win/win?

Interdependence Enables Synergy

G oogle defines *synergy* as, "The interaction or cooperation of two or more organizations, substances, or other agents to produce a combined effect greater than the sum of their separate effects."

With regard to human problem-solving, a beneficial *synergistic* effect occurs when *divergent* ideas or perspectives combine to produce a solution. This happens when a mindset of win/lose independency shifts to win/win interdependency. This is much easier said than done, as you realize when referring to politics.

Note the modifier *divergent* used when defining a synergistic effect from group decision-making. If everyone on a problem-solving team has similar expertise, problem-solving viewpoints, and educational backgrounds consensual agreement on a solution will be relatively quick, but the outcome will reflect only the sum of similar parts.

A synergistic action plan occurs when the parts are dissimilar and interact to produce an innovative solution which might be a compromise between divergent perspectives. Reaching a consensus or compromise between participants with various disparate opinions does not happen efficiently, but the resulting action plan will likely be most effective.

Perhaps a discussion of politics is illustrative of maximum disparity, and unlikely consensus-building and synergy. Indeed, that's why people are frequently advised, "Don't discuss politics." It's apparently assumed that people cannot be open-minded with regard to politically charged issues. While discussing politics will likely not change opinions, it does enable an understanding and appreciation of divergent viewpoints.

A win/lose mindset prevents open dialogue and constructive sharing of opinions and potential solutions. Subsequent life lessons reveal human dynamics that contribute to this unfortunate situation and suggest strategies for a) activating appreciation of divergent perspectives, b) building consensus, and c) achieving synergy.

Thinking Beyond the Illustration

Directions: Based on what you have read for this life lesson, respond to the questions below.

1. What barriers prevent a win/win problem-solving approach between two divergent groups, like Democrats versus Republicans?
2. What does this phrase mean: "The whole is greater than the sum of its parts"?

Responding to the Illustration

Directions: Look at the illustration above. Refer to this illustration to answer the following questions.

1. What does this illustration mean to you?
2. What does the decision-making depicted in the illustration suggest with regard to leadership and interpersonal trust?
3. How could a group leader inhibit such inconsistency between private thinking and group behavior?

LIFE LESSON 22

Watch Out for Groupthink

G*roupthink* refers to a tendency for groups to reach a quick decision without taking the time for substantial discussion. Sometimes the leader of the group actually stifles disagreement and advocates unanimity in order to make a quick decision and move the meeting along. In such cases, people are unlikely to challenge peers or colleagues for fear of losing status or friendships. The result is a deterioration of thoughtful decision-making, practical considerations, and moral judgment.

A well-known and tragic example of *groupthink* was the space shuttle *Challenger* disaster on January 28, 1986. The entire crew of seven died as a result of an explosion on the space shuttle. The likely cause of this disaster was a malfunction of the rocket seals due to the freezing temperature. Although the engineers of the rocket booster anticipated a possible seal problem, the NASA management team denied the engineers' warnings and agreed with the executive order to launch the *Challenger*.

This group decision, as well as other historical fiascoes such as the failure to anticipate the Japanese attack on Pearl Harbor, The Bay of Pigs Invasion of Cuba, the escalation of the Vietnam War, the Watergate cover-up, the Iran-Contra affair, and the Chernobyl-reactor tragedy resulted from teams of well-intentioned professionals making unwise and risky groupthink decisions.

When a group leader embraces diverse opinions, invites input and critique, and challenges individuals to "think outside the box," s/he decreases the probability of groupthink. Leaders who admit vulnerability, own up to their mistakes, and solicit corrective feedback set the stage for continuous improvement and naturally stifle groupthink.

Of course, the degree of diversity of opinions, educational backgrounds, personal experiences, and demographics determine the ease of preventing groupthink and benefiting from synergistic decision-making. This is the theme of the next two life lessons—Life Lessons 23 and 24.

Thinking Beyond the Illustration

Directions: Based on what you have read for this life lesson, respond to the questions below.

1. How could a group leader facilitate genuine consensus?
2. Can you recall a time when your behavior indicated agreement with members of a group but your thoughts suggested some disagreement? Please explain.

Responding to the Illustration

Directions: Look at the illustration above. Refer to this illustration to answer the following questions.

1. Why is the hunter unlikely to get a fair trial?
2. What aspects of the illustration facilitate the occurrence of *groupthink*?
3. How would you change the illustration to introduce diversity and enable a fair trial?

Diversity Optimizes Synergy

A high-performance team includes people with knowledge, skills, and abilities that complement each other's competencies. They understand that group decision-making and participation benefit from diversity, even though obtaining consensus from a diverse group is relatively cumbersome and time consuming. They realize that the synergistic results of individual contributions increase as a function of the diversity of ideas, opinions, and mindsets among the participants.

As addressed in Life Lesson 21, all of this is easier said than done. It's more efficient and convenient to just sit back and go along, giving up individual identity and a sense of personal responsibility. This is analogous to the diffusion of responsibility phenomenon that is used to explain the *bystander effect*—the observation that the more people present at an emergency, the less likely any one person will help.[24]

A key challenge for a group facilitator or team leader is making diversity work well to obtain optimal synergy. Innovative ideas and solutions to problems can only emerge from new combinations of divergent competencies, experiences, paradigms, and, yes, biases. This level of interactive dialogue and interpersonal learning leads to optimal synergy: Perspectives and life experiences mixing and matching to activate a creative birth and death of ideas—perspectives and experiences evolving into a whole of greater understanding and innovation.

The whole is greater than the sum of its diverse parts, not only because there's *synergy* between the parts, but also because the parts contribute to the whole and manifest its essence, its purpose, its function. Thus, the whole has a fundamental relationship to its parts. Indeed, the whole (the group or team) is the reason for the existence of its parts.

A healthy family, school system, organization, or community must actively care for its members in order to function well. Thus, the diverse parts of an effective whole have synergistic relations between each other and with the whole.

Thinking Beyond the Illustration

Directions: Based on what you have read for this life lesson, respond to the questions below.

1. What are advantages (if any) and disadvantages (if any) of group decision-making among individuals with similar viewpoints, values, and political orientation?
2. Are you a member of a group, team, or committee that benefits from diversity and/or that could benefit from more diversity? Please explain.

Responding to the Illustration

Directions: Look at the illustration above. Refer to this illustration to answer the following questions.

1. What does this illustration mean to you?
2. What attitudes are displayed by the individuals in this illustration, and what could be reasons for the happy versus unhappy faces?
3. Given a simple definition of a system as "a set of connected things or parts forming a complex whole," how is your body a system? How about your family?

The Power of Systems Thinking

D on't blame people for problems caused by the system."[25] This profound quotation from W. Edwards Deming reminds us to focus our efforts on optimizing the system.[26] In other words, when assessing, analyzing, or solving a problem, attempt to see the big picture. Behavior is influenced by many interdependent dispositional and situational factors, and the occurrence of a particular behavior can affect the various person-states and environmental factors of a system.

Take the common behavior of driving a vehicle, for example, and consider an independent versus an interdependent focus and its impact on behavior and attitude. It seems too many drivers are not systems thinkers—they demonstrate an individualistic, win/lose attitude rather than the win/win cooperative mindset needed to optimize the system. They dart back and forth between lanes, often without signaling, just to shave a few seconds off their trip time. Given a line of vehicles in the left lane, these drivers pass the vehicles on the right and then use their left-turn signal to squeeze in front of the line.

How about those slow drivers clogging up the left lane, perhaps because they'll eventually make a left-hand turn several miles ahead? Then we have the drivers who use a cell phone while driving and take extra time at intersections because they are reading or sending a text message. These drivers are also displaying an individualist win/lose perspective—perhaps unconsciously or unintentionally—which makes the transportation system less efficient and less effective.

It's likely few of these drivers consider their impact on the overall system—a system that works best when everyone follows the same rules, norms, and courtesies of the road. Perhaps the driver in the left lane who allows space for the self-serving driver who passed the line of vehicles on the right sees the bigger picture and realizes how a simple AC4P act of considerate driving helps to optimize the system.

So how can the function of an organization, community, or family system be optimized? One way: *Understand*, *practice*, and *teach* others the evidence-based life lessons in this Life-COACH manual.

Thinking Beyond the Illustration

Directions: Based on what you have read for this life lesson, respond to the questions below.

1. How do Life Lessons 19, 20, and 21 on interdependency and synergy relate to this life lesson?
2. What are the advantages of maintaining an interdependent systems mindset—becoming a **systems thinker**?

Responding to the Illustration

Directions: Look at the illustration above. Refer to this illustration to answer the following questions.

1. What does the illustration mean to you?
2. Can you remember a time when you received directions to do something with no explanation or rationale for the behavior asked of you? Please explain, including whether you followed the request and how you felt.
3. Why is it a good idea to offer a reason or a rationale for a rule or behavioral request?

LIFE LESSON 25

The Power of Feeling Empowered

Empowerment is a popular term in the work world, typically referring to the delegation of authority or responsibility. Sometimes this term is used in educational or home settings. When supervisors, teachers, or parents say, "I empower you," they really mean, "Get 'er done." As reflected in the illustration for this life lesson, the message is, "Make it happen; no questions asked." Without an explanation or rationale for such an assignment, this approach could be perceived as top-down control and could influence contrary behavior, as discussed in Life Lesson 16.

The connection between *empowerment* and *self-motivation* becomes obvious when considering how a parent, teacher, coach, or supervisor could assess whether an individual *feels* empowered. Ask these three questions to determine whether another person (or yourself) feels empowered regarding a particular assignment: a) "Can you do it?" b) "Will it work?" and c) "Is it worth it?"[27]

A "No" response to the first question implies a need for **training** (i.e., behavioral practice with feedback), whereas a "No" response to the second question reflects a need for **education** to explain the connection between completing the assignment and a relevant mission or long-term **vision** of the individual, group, or organization. For example, you might need to explain how completing an assignment can lead to a commendable course grade, a team win, or the achievement of an *AC4P culture*.

"Is it worth it?" is a *motivational* question, and a "Yes" answer indicates that the participant believes the consequence or outcome resulting from accomplishing the task is worth the effort. This might require a discussion of long-term consequences and even a presentation of evidence (i.e., data) to show eventual consequences that can result from effort comparable to that required for completing the target task.

This motivational belief can be difficult to develop and maintain if a long-term delayed outcome (e.g., the prevention of an unintentional and improbable injury) seems insufficient to justify the performance of inconvenient and/or uncomfortable behavior (e.g., the routine use of personal protective equipment).

Thinking Beyond the Illustration

Directions: Based on what you have read for this life lesson, respond to the questions below.

1. What does it mean to feel empowered?
2. How does feeling empowered relate to feeling self-motivated? In other words, how are the person-states of feeling empowered and self-motivated similar and/or different?

Responding to the Illustration

Directions: Look at the illustration above. Refer to this illustration to answer the following questions.

1. What mistake has Mom made in this communication with her son?
2. Can you recall a conversation when you came on strong with your opinion or position before considering the other person's stance or position? Please explain.
3. Why is it best to understand another individual's opinion or perspective before stating your own?

LIFE LESSON 26

Communicate with Empathy

S eek first to understand before being understood." This profound quotation from Stephen R. Covey reflects a most important concept to understand and practice in order to achieve a level of interpersonal discourse most likely to appreciate and improve human dynamics.[28]

Whether the topic is *empathic* listening, *empathic* discipline, or *empathic* leadership, the focus is on the other person's feelings, needs, or perceptions. When we begin our conversations with this approach, we can customize our presentation to fit the other person's perspective and, consequently, be most successful at getting our point across.

When observing another individual's behavior, try to view the context and circumstances from that person's perspective. When you listen to explanations or excuses for less-than-optimal behavior, try to see yourself in the same situation. Imagine what defense mechanism you might use to protect your ego or self-esteem. And when considering an action plan for improvement, try to view various alternatives though the eyes of the other person.

Please recall the *nondirective stance* introduced in Life Lesson 8, and reflect on the advice to first ask questions. We should hear every word of the answers to our questions and look for attitudes, emotions, and commitment reflected by body language and manner of expression as much as by the words themselves.

When you maintain the mindset that there's more than one side to every story, you might find another person's perspective to be very different than yours. And if you listen with empathy to the rationale (or excuses) for a contrary opinion or behavior, you might gain appreciation for the diversity displayed and enhance mutual respect.

An empathic level of awareness and appreciation is not easy to achieve. It can only be reached by minimizing those reactive filters that bias our conversations before we can listen actively and *empathically* to communication from another person. Through empathic listening we prepare ourselves to act on behalf of another person's well-being.

Thinking Beyond the Illustration

Directions: Based on what you have read for this life lesson, respond to the questions below.

1. What does the term **empathy** mean to you?
2. Do you perceive a difference between *empathy* and *sympathy*? Please explain.

Responding to the Illustration

Directions: Look at the illustration above. Refer to this illustration to answer the following questions.

1. Why is the boy holding a paper with an A+ grade unhappy?
2. Why does the boy believe he will be beat up by other boys in his class?
3. What could the teacher who is shaking the boy's hand and giving him public recognition in front of his class have done to prevent the boy's negative emotion and from being the victim of bullying behavior?

LIFE LESSON 27

Live by the Platinum Rule

"Praise publicly and reprimand privately." Does this popular slogan sound like good common sense? Don't most people want to be praised publicly most of the time? Not necessarily, because some people feel embarrassed when singled out in front of a group, as depicted in the illustration for this life lesson. Part of this embarrassment could be fear of subsequent harassment by peers.

Certainly, the deliverer of public recognition believes the experience will be special and positive for the recipient of the praise. In this case, the person delivering the public praise would probably prefer to receive such recognition in a public setting. This is an example of the *Golden Rule*—"Treat others the way you want to be treated."

However, the illustration suggests that some individuals dislike receiving public recognition delivered by parents, friends, teachers, coaches, work supervisors, or public officials. Does this example discredit the Golden Rule, at least to some extent?

Better than the Golden Rule is the *Platinum Rule*—"Treat others the way *they* want to be treated."[29] In other words, before administering a particular "treatment" (e.g., recognition ceremony, intervention technique, or disciplinary policy) solicit suggestions and opinions from those affected by the "treatment." Notice how the Platinum Rule connects directly to Life Lesson 26 on the power of empathy.

Considering another person's perspective with empathy also enhances the perception of personal choice, as we discussed in Life Lesson 17. To treat others the way they want to be treated you need to solicit their opinion, or perhaps give them a choice between alternative interventions, policies, or behavior-management techniques. Implementing the Platinum Rule facilitates the perception of choice among those being "treated," and this fuels self-motivation.

As Dr. Deming taught us years ago, "People support that which they helped to create."[25] Solicit intervention suggestions from the target individual(s) and you'll enhance the relevance and beneficial impact of the intervention.

Thinking Beyond the Illustration

Directions: Based on what you have read for this life lesson, respond to the questions below.

1. Recall a time when you were praised or recognized in front of a group. How did you feel?
2. Would you rather be praised publicly or privately by a parent, teacher, coach, or supervisor?

Responding to the Illustration

Directions: Look at the illustration above. Refer to this illustration to answer the following questions.

1. What is the family story behind this illustration?
2. How does this illustration reflect the common phrase, "What goes around, comes around"?
3. Although this illustration of the **Reciprocity Principle** shows unwanted behavior and an unhappy Mom, are there situations where this "pay-it-forward" principle can lead to desirable behavior and a positive attitude? Please explain.

LIFE LESSON 28

The Power of Reciprocity

The phrase, "Do for me and I'll do for you" reflects the *Reciprocity Principle* of social influence.[15] When you're nice to others, they'll feel obligated to do something nice for you. Many charitable organizations include a small gift in their solicitation package (e.g., personal return-address labels, a calendar, a pen, or a small writing pad), assuming the recipient will feel obligated to return the favor with a financial donation.

Recall Life Lesson 24 on *systems thinking*. A systems thinker sees the bigger picture and realizes that a personal favor might be returned to someone other than the original performer of the actively-caring-for-people (AC4P) behavior. Systems thinkers also consider the benefits of *vicarious reciprocity*—when an observer of AC4P behavior is inspired through observational learning to perform prosocial AC4P behavior (Life Lessons 13 & 14).

Systems thinkers (Life Lesson 24) realize that their reaction to people who do them a favor can either stifle or mobilize a spiral of interpersonal reciprocity. For example, when systems thinkers receive a "Thank you" for their AC4P behavior they do not demean the favor by saying something like, "No problem" or, "It was really nothing." This can make the AC4P behavior appear trivial and reduce the impetus for follow-up reciprocity or pay-it-forward behavior.

Systems thinkers avoid demeaning their AC4P acts of kindness. They react to a "Thank you" with something like, "You're very welcome, but I know you'd do the same for me." This shows genuine admiration for the "Thank you" and increases the likelihood more "Thank you's" will be given. Plus, this reply supports the *Reciprocity Principle* and perhaps increases the occurrence of more pay-it-forward AC4P behavior.

With this social-influence *Principle of Reciprocity*, systems thinkers appreciate how a small change in verbal behavior can encourage more AC4P behavior—not only from the recipients of a kind act, but also from those who observe or hear about the positive AC4P interaction (e.g., *vicarious reciprocity*).

Thinking Beyond the Illustration

Directions: Based on what you have read for this life lesson, respond to the questions below.

1. Have you ever wanted to pass on an act of kindness you received? Please explain.
2. How could this life lesson contribute to cultivating an *actively-caring-for-people (AC4P)* culture?

Responding to the Illustration

Directions: Look at the illustration above. Refer to this illustration to answer the following questions.

1. What does this illustration mean to you?
2. Suppose a homeless person asks you for ten dollars and you say "No." After accepting your rejection the beggar asks, "How about only one dollar?" Would you be more likely to give this person a dollar than if the first request was for a dollar? Please explain your answer.
3. Why is this life lesson referred to as the ***Door-in-the-Face technique***?

LIFE LESSON 29

The Door-in-the-Face Technique

D r. Robert Cialdini and associates were among the first to demonstrate the influence of this social-influence principle.[30] Posing as representatives of a youth counseling program, they approached college students on campus and requested their volunteer service to chaperon a group of juvenile delinquents on a day trip to the zoo. When this was the first and only request, four of the 24 students they approached volunteered to help.

However, three times more students volunteered when the researchers *first* asked for a much larger favor. They first asked whether the student would be willing to counsel juvenile delinquents for two hours a week over a two-year period.

All of the students refused this request, but then half of these individuals volunteered to serve as unpaid chaperons for a day at the zoo. Apparently, the researchers' willingness to retreat from their initial request influenced several students to *reciprocate* and comply with a smaller request.

Now, suppose someone asks you for a thousand dollars and then follows up with a request for one dollar. Would you give up the dollar? Research evidence suggests a small request is likely to be declined if the initial request is too large.[31] Perhaps the dramatic contrast between requests seems manipulative and illegitimate. If the recipient of a request senses an attempt to control his or her behavior, a challenge to personal choice is activated (Life Lesson 16) and any influence of the *Reciprocity Principle* is stifled.

So why do lawyers ask for outlandish amounts of money at the start of a civil trial? And, why do labor negotiators start with extreme demands? Perhaps these agents of influence do not expect to receive their initial request, but they have learned that they are more likely to succeed with a second more realistic request after retreating from the first. Through real-world negotiation, they have learned the power of this reciprocity-based door-in-the-face technique.

Thinking Beyond the Illustration

Directions: Based on what you have read for this life lesson, respond to the questions below.

1. How does this life lesson relate to a lawyer's request for an outlandish amount of money at the start of a civil trial?
2. How does this life lesson connect to Life Lesson 28 on the *Principle of Reciprocity*?

Responding to the Illustration

Directions: Look at the illustration above. Refer to this illustration to answer the following questions.

1. What does this illustration mean to you?
2. Suppose a homeless person asks you for 25 cents, and since you have a quarter in your pocket you hand it over to the beggar with a smile. He thanks you and then asks, "Could you make it an even dollar bill?" Would you be more likely to give this person a dollar than if his first request was for a dollar? Please explain.
3. Why is this technique referred to as *Foot-in-the-Door*?

LIFE LESSON 30

The Foot-in-the-Door Technique

The **Principle of Consistency**—the need for congruence between what we think, how we feel, and what we do—fuels this social influence technique. We experience tension or **cognitive dissonance** when we perceive a lack of consistency between a behavior we choose to perform and another behavior, attitude, or value.[32] The key word in that sentence is *choose*. If we feel coerced into doing something, we will not feel uncomfortable if that behavior is inconsistent with a personal attitude, value, or another behavior.[33]

So in order to be consistent, a person who chooses to follow a small request is likely to comply with a larger request later.[34] For example, after a child or roommate agrees to make his/her bed, s/he is more likely to comply with a larger request, like cleaning an entire room or washing the dishes.

Because of the Consistency Principle, an intervention that successfully changes someone's behavior can influence the individual's attitude, or vice versa. Effective behavioral therapy *acts* a person into related *thinking*, whereas successful cognitive therapy *thinks* a person into performing *behavior* consistent with the new cognition(s).

The Consistency Principle is also responsible for the power of **social labeling**, which is evident when an individual is assigned an ability, attribute, attitude, or belief.[35] For example, labeling a driver as a careful and safe driver can increase the frequency of his/her safe-driving behaviors. But of course, the label "reckless-driver" may prompt the driver to take more risks behind the wheel.

The seminal research by Carol Dweck indicates the need to use effort- or behavior-related labels for a desirable characteristic (e.g., "she tries hard" rather than "she is gifted"), because labels that imply a fixed ability rather than growth potential can stifle motivation to take on challenges.[36] A person with a fixed ability label is apt to resist volunteering for a challenging project with self-talk such as, "If I accept this challenge and fail, people's positive perceptions of my special ability will decrease."

Thinking Beyond the Illustration

Directions: Based on what you have read for this life lesson, respond to the questions below.

1. Have you ever made a commitment to contribute time, money, and/or effort for a particular undertaking and were later asked to contribute even more? Please explain. Did your initial smaller contribution motivate (or obligate) you to contribute more?
2. How does effective education connect to this life lesson?

Responding to the Illustration

Directions: Look at the illustration above. Refer to this illustration to answer the following questions.

1. What does this illustration mean to you?
2. Although the judge's statement is likely viewed as silly or ridiculous, do you see a grain of truth here? Please explain.
3. Where and when have you resisted changing your opinion or viewpoint in the face of opposing information?

LIFE LESSON 31

Consistency Fuels Commitment

Many psychologists consider the *Principle of Consistency* a weapon of influence lying deep within us and directing our everyday actions. It reflects our motivation to be (and appear) consistent. People feel pressure to be consistent from three sources: a) society values **consistency** in people, b) consistent conduct builds interpersonal trust and is beneficial to daily interactions with others, and c) a consistent orientation allows for shortcuts in information processing and decision-making.[15]

Instead of taking the time and effort to consider all the relevant information before making a particular decision, people only need to remember their prior commitment or related decision and respond consistently. The *Consistency Principle* explains people's resistance to change, while also suggesting ways to motivate lasting improvement in both behavior and attitude.

Let's consider the **hypocrisy effect** as an intervention to motivate the occurrence of a desirable target behavior. Ask participants to think about what they have done versus what they believe they should do.[37] The intervention process is as follows:

A. Give one or more participants a convincing rationale for a desirable behavior (e.g., when crossing a street in the pedestrian crosswalk support an *AC4P culture* by waving a positive sign of gratitude to the driver(s) who stopped for you).
B. Ask the participant(s) to commit to performing the desirable behavior whenever it's warranted by the situation.
C. Ask the participant(s) to list the most recent times they did not perform the desirable behavior of their chosen commitment.

In a sense, this technique activates a *guilt trip*. Individuals realize an inconsistency between their prior actions and a current belief or attribute that led to a behavioral commitment. Psychologists call awareness of a behavior-attitude discrepancy *cognitive dissonance*.[32] Whatever the label, this process reflects an effective application of this life lesson—"thinking a person into a certain action or behavior."

Thinking Beyond the Illustration

Directions: Based on what you have read for this life lesson, respond to the questions below.

1. When is commitment to a particular perspective good? When is resistance to change not so good?
2. What viewpoint(s) or opinion(s) do you have that would be difficult to change? Please explain.

61

Responding to the Illustration

Directions: Look at the illustration above. Refer to this illustration to answer the following questions.

1. Is there any possibility the driver in the illustration would follow the orders of his boss in the back seat? Why or why not?
2. Have you ever observed people following the directions of an authority person when the request was counter to common sense and/or human welfare? Please explain.
3. Have you ever followed the orders of an authority figure (e.g., a parent, teacher, coach, or boss) without questioning the legitimacy of the request? Please explain.

LIFE LESSON 32

The Power of Authority

From childhood through adulthood, we learn to follow legitimate authority—from "mother knows best" to "the boss knows best." This gives us an excuse to avoid taking personal responsibility for what we are doing. If someone with authority tells you to take a risk, you can comply with a clear conscience—"If something goes wrong, it won't be my fault. He told me to do it."

The term *authority* has negative connotations because many historical examples and research in psychological science have illustrated the top-down coercive influence of people abusing their power of authority, as displayed during the Holocaust.

In the 1960s, Stanley Milgram and associates demonstrated that 65 percent of intelligent and well-meaning college students followed orders to administer 450-volt electric shocks to a screaming peer.[38]

Even Milgram was surprised that so many of his subjects, ranging in age from 20 to 50, obeyed the experimenter's "shocking" requests, concluding that, "Ordinary people, simply doing their jobs, and without any particular hostility on their part, can become agents in a terrible destructive process."[39] Relatedly, people might overlook obvious safety hazards and put themselves and others at risk with the self-talk, "I'm just following orders."

However, many people with authority (e.g., physicians, ministers, teachers, and parents) activate *desirable* behaviors. People use safety devices, take vitamin pills and supplements, follow security precautions, and get periodic medical exams because one or more persons with credible authority told them to perform those behaviors.

We rarely perceive an immediate health or safety benefit from complying with such prevention advice, but we take the word of an authority figure that such behavior will pay off in the long run.

Hence, the power of authority has both beneficial and debilitating consequences to human well-being and welfare, depending upon who has the authority.

Thinking Beyond the Illustration

Directions: Based on what you have read for this life lesson, respond to the questions below.

1. What behaviors do you perform regularly for your safety, security, and/or health because someone told you to do so?
2. What are the advantages and disadvantages of the **Authority Principle**—the tendency to comply with a request from a person with credible authority?

Responding to the Illustration

Directions: Look at the illustration above. Refer to this illustration to answer the following questions.

1. Why did the representative of ABC win the contract?
2. In your opinion, which slogan is more true: "Unlikes attract" or "Birds of a feather flock together"? Please explain your choice.
3. In what ways are you similar to and different from a best friend?

LIFE LESSON 33

The Attraction to Similarities

We like people who are like us. Hence, it's a myth that "Opposites (or unlikes) attract." Rather, "Birds of a feather flock together." People tend to like people who are similar to them, and they are more likely to comply with requests from these individuals.[15] Of course, the types of similarities vary dramatically—from comparable opinions and attributes to educational and nurturing backgrounds and past experiences, attire, and notable behaviors.

This similarity principle comes into play when people modify their attire to be more acceptable to audiences, like when males wear or remove a tie in order to appear more similar to the group. Likewise, when we mention acquaintances whom the other person knows and respects, we are showing the kind of similarity that can increase liking.

Employing similarities is one evidence-based technique to increase appreciation for another person and thereby decrease interpersonal conflict and bullying.[40] Two other research-validated ways to establish a context of relational appreciation and attraction were covered in prior lessons: give praise (Life Lessons 8 & 9) and promote interdependency (Life Lessons 20 & 21).

Not only does behavioral recognition enhance a perception of competence and fuel self-motivation, it increases attraction—in both directions. The person you recognize likes you more because you noticed behavior worthy of giving that person supportive feedback, and you appreciate this person more because you noticed this person's commendable behavior. This mutual ingratiation increases feelings of belongingness and interdependency. Then, through the power of reciprocity (Life Lesson 28), one interpersonal recognition can lead to more recognition and more ingratiation throughout a culture.

Social psychologists have tracked increases in interpersonal attraction when individuals transition from competitive to cooperative situations. Because you've been there, this seems like basic common sense: The greater the perception of interdependency toward the achievement of a common goal, the greater the interpersonal attraction.

Thinking Beyond the Illustration

Directions: Based on what you have read for this life lesson, respond to the questions below.

1. When you first meet someone, what qualities do you look for to determine if you will get along and perhaps become good friends?
2. What do you do (or what could you do) to increase good feelings between people and prevent interpersonal conflict or bullying?

Responding to the Illustration

Directions: Look at the illustration above. Refer to this illustration to answer the following questions.

1. What does this illustration mean to you?
2. What does the female driver intend by shouting, "Pig"?
3. Why does the male driver yell, "Road Hog"?

LIFE LESSON 34

All Perception Is Selective

It's likely most readers have heard the term **selective perception**, and perhaps have used this concept to explain a misunderstanding or a *misperception*. Please consider this: The term *selective perception* is redundant because all perception is selective—biased by past experience, as well as both dispositional (nature) and situational (nurture) factors.

Recall our discussion in Life Lesson 1 that our behavior is influenced by both nature and nurture. Well, the same is true for our perceptions. Simply put, perception is an individual's interpretation of a sensation that is experienced through any or all of the five senses (i.e., what we see, hear, feel, smell, and/or taste). Thus, the Sensation-Perception course offered by the psychology department at many colleges and universities covers both the physiology of our sensory system (i.e., sensation) and the factors that influence our interpretation of sensation (i.e., perception).

Let's consider how the illustration for this life lesson reflects the concept of **premature cognitive commitment**, introduced by Ellen J. Langer in her book—*Mindfulness*.[41] Specifically, the biased perception of the male driver has made him mindless of the road hazard ahead of him as well as the attempt of the female driver to warn him.

Why is this premature cognitive commitment? First, it is *premature*—occurring before adequate diagnosis, analysis, and decision-making. Second, it is *cognitive*—a thinking process that influences perception, attitude, and behavior. Finally, it is a *commitment*—a relatively permanent perspective or mindset that filters the information we receive, biases our interpretation, and shapes how we act.

In other words, we often commit ourselves to an initial impression without the benefit of critical thinking. Daniel Kahneman refers to this thinking as System 1 (reactive) rather than System 2 (reflective).[42] This contributes greatly to disagreement and conflict between people. In addition, our perception is tainted by critical attributional errors or biases—explained in the next three life lessons.

Thinking Beyond the Illustration

Directions: Based on what you have read for this life lesson, respond to the questions below.

1. Why does the dog in the illustration understand the female's warning better than the male driver?
2. Have you ever experienced or observed a situation analogous to the illustration where people's verbal behavior reflected differences in perception? Please explain.

Responding to the Illustration

Directions: Look at the illustration above. Refer to this illustration to answer the following questions.

1. Why is it difficult for the dogs to understand the behavior of the runners?
2. How often and when do you attempt to understand your own behavior by asking yourself, "Why did I do that?"
3. Do you attempt to understand the behavior of others with a question like, "Why did he or she do that?"

Biases of Attribution

Attempting to understand or account for the behavior of others is a daily cognitive process for many people. Parents try to understand the inappropriate behavior of their children in order to devise a corrective action plan. Teachers strive to interpret the successes and failures of their students in order to improve their instructional methods. Coaches attempt to identify factors that influence certain skills of their athletes. Supervisors are continuously comparing the performance of wage workers to make job assignments and promotional decisions.

These assessments are often documented. They can be found in an individual's personnel file or résumé—as commentary on a student's report card or on an employee's annual performance appraisal, and in letters of recommendation for a candidate's application for a job, an opportunity for advanced education, or for an achievement award. Question: Are these evaluations fair and unbiased?

Life Lesson 34 on selective perception indicates one type of evaluation bias. Let's consider another source of prejudice: ***attributional bias***. Suppose you need to evaluate two persons who objectively have achieved the same outcomes. However, you believe one of these individuals did not contribute maximum effort but sometimes loafed along. In contrast, the other person is seemingly less talented and reached this level of output by working much harder. Would you give each of these individuals the same performance evaluation?

Research indicates most people would assign a higher rating to the second individual—the one who showed the most effort and exceeded expectations.[43] Is this fair? If the evaluation is for work output only, subjective attributional judgments are irrelevant and should not influence a performance evaluation. Besides, attributional judgments are biased by a limited sampling of behavior and the observer's *selective perception* (Life Lesson 34).

But there is more. The next two life lessons explain additional attributional biases that can dramatically distort our evaluations of others and make assessments unfair.

Thinking Beyond the Illustration

Directions: Based on what you have read for this life lesson, respond to the questions below.

1. What factors could bias your analysis of your own behavior?
2. What factors could bias your evaluation of the behavior of another person?

Responding to the Illustration

Directions: Look at the illustration above. Refer to this illustration to answer the following questions.

1. What does this illustration mean to you?
2. Which individual is attributing situational factors to golfing, and who is explaining the performance with dispositional (or nature) factors?
3. What negative consequences could result from a misattribution of the causes of another person's behavior?

LIFE LESSON 36

The Fundamental Attribution Error

The *fundamental attribution error* is the tendency for people to automatically attribute the observed behavior of another person to that person's nature, character, innate abilities, personality traits, or—in one word—*disposition*.[44] We overemphasize other people's internal attributes to explain their behavior, and we often ignore the fact that situations play a significant role in determining their behavior. This bias is called "fundamental" because it's virtually universal, and it's an "error" because such judgments are frequently wrong. It reflects a lack of systems thinking (Life Lesson 24).

This fundamental bias occurs often in industry when "investigating" the cause of an injury to an employee. Supervisors and safety professionals are apt to blame characteristics of the worker for the mishap. Failing to consider the influence of the situation or context, they think or say, "He was careless or risky." In fact, a primary criticism of behavior-based safety (BBS)[2]—a worldwide application of behavioral science to prevent injuries—has been the *inaccurate* presumption that BBS blames workers for their injuries without considering the broader context of situational factors.

If a vehicle cuts in front of you on the road, you will likely make an automatic negative judgment of the driver. You may think or actually shout, "What a jerk!" You make this negative attribution because you think only a "jerk" would cut you off.

But, suppose you inadvertently cut somebody off. You probably don't think, "I'm a jerk!" More than likely you would think some situational factor caused your behavior. Perhaps you were distracted by another vehicle or an unfamiliar traffic pattern. You wouldn't think that you didn't care about the safety of others.

This focus on *situational determinants* of your road-safety error is analogous to the golfer in the illustration who is attributing his poor "driving" behavior to the environment—wind, high grass, and inadequate equipment. This reflects another error of attribution addressed in the next life lesson—the *self-serving bias*.

Thinking Beyond the Illustration

Directions: Based on what you have read for this life lesson, respond to the questions below.

1. What dispositional and situational factors might influence the occurrence of interpersonal bullying?
2. Recall a time when your *undesirable* behavior was evaluated by another person. What factors were considered in this negative evaluation, and what factors were missed that could have resulted in another conclusion?

Responding to the Illustration

Directions: Look at the illustration above. Refer to this illustration to answer the following questions.

1. How does the illustration demonstrate a *self-serving bias*?
2. Given the *fundamental attribution error*, what is the store clerk thinking regarding the reason for the injury?
3. Recall a time when you were disappointed in your performance (e.g., not doing well on an exam, a group presentation, or a performance appraisal). How did you explain this subpar performance to yourself and to others?

LIFE LESSON 37

The Self-Serving Bias

The *self-serving bias* is an attributional process whereby people explain their behavior—successful or unsuccessful—for personal advantage.[45] They explain their performance to enhance or protect their self-esteem. We maintain positive views of ourselves by blaming bad outcomes on features of the situation, unless self-blame is unavoidable. In contrast, when things go well, we attribute success to our skills, abilities, and/or positive aspects of our personality, unless self-praise is not plausible.

A self-serving bias in moderate doses can be useful because it protects our self-esteem. However, if we consistently disregard the negative or less-than-optimal aspects of a reasonably objective self-assessment and keep blaming the situation for our errors or our suboptimal performance, others may come to view us as excuse-makers and/or arrogant.

More importantly, if we resist or deny dispositional attributes or personal responsibilities for an observation of our subpar performance, we can stifle considerations and opportunities for personal improvement. If people have made regular deposits in our "people-relations" bank account by giving us supportive feedback for our commendable behavior (Life Lesson 8), we can readily accept corrective feedback—a withdrawal from our "people-relations" bank account—and adjust our behavior for continuous improvement.

When another person does something negative or performs below expectations, an onlooker typically attributes that person's behavior to a negative disposition (e.g., the golfer in Life Lesson 36). But when we fail or underperform, we tend to blame the situation (e.g., the hammer-returner in Life Lesson 37).

Note how the combination of Life Lessons 36 and 37 can bias the results of an investigation of a classroom conflict, a family dispute, a vehicle crash, or a workplace injury. While the vehicle driver will attribute the mishap to a list of situational factors, observers of the incident will likely place primary blame on dispositional characteristics of the driver.

Thinking Beyond the Illustration

Directions: Based on what you have read for this life lesson, respond to the questions below.

1. What are the advantages (if any) and disadvantages (if any) of attributing your poor performance to *situational* rather than *dispositional* factors?
2. Recall a time when your performance was stellar (e.g., on an exam, in a sports competition, or on a performance evaluation). How did you explain that success to yourself and to others?

Negative Thoughts Can Make You Miss.

Responding to the Illustration

Directions: Look at the illustration above. Refer to this illustration to answer the following questions.

1. How did **self-talk** influence the behavior of the basketball athlete?
2. How has your self-talk *facilitated* successful performance and/or *inhibited* successful performance?
3. How can self-talk set the stage for *success seeking* or *failure avoiding* (Life Lesson 10)?

Self-Talk Can Help or Hurt

A behavioral scientist defines thinking as covert behavior or *self-talk*. And, there's plenty of empirical evidence that intrapersonal conversation or self-talk about a task can facilitate or stifle success. This is common sense to most readers because you've been there. You understand how the self-talk of the basketball player in the illustration put her in a failure-avoiding mindset and influenced the missed shot. It's just another demonstration of the *self-fulfilling prophecy*.[46]

Our expectations influence our performance. Note, however, that an intrapersonal conversation does not need to specify an expectation of failure. Self-talk can support success seeking over failure avoiding. Just suggesting a positive rather than a negative outcome can be enough to facilitate success.

Consider how our self-talk both influences and reflects our self-esteem. In fact, it could be said that our mental script about ourselves *is* our self-esteem. We can focus our intrapersonal conversations on the good or bad things other people say about us. Indeed, our self-esteem can go up or down according to how we talk to ourselves about the way others talk about us.

Note the critical connection between self-talk and feeling empowered (Lesson 25). We feel empowered when we believe a) we can do the task, b) the task is relevant to our mission or ultimate *vision*, and c) completing the task is worth the effort. How do we acquire and sustain the beliefs necessary to feel empowered?

I bet you already realize that the three empowerment beliefs—*self-efficacy*, **response-efficacy**, and **outcome expectancy** (Life Lesson 25)—are developed, nourished, and sustained through our self-talk. Of course, our self-talk can also deny, disregard, or oppose these empowerment-determining beliefs. A failure-avoiding or failure-accepting mindset can inhibit perceptions of competence and a prophecy of success.

Thinking Beyond the Illustration

Directions: Based on what you have read for this life lesson, respond to the questions below.

1. What should a person say to himself or herself in order to feel more self-motivated about accepting a particular challenge?
2. Recall and explain a personal experience whereby your self-talk might have influenced your performance (e.g., on an exam or for a public speech, athletic event, or job assignment).

Responding to the Illustration

Directions: Look at the illustration above. Refer to this illustration to answer the following questions.

1. What emotional differences are the two runners experiencing in the illustration?
2. What does it mean to have "butterflies" in our stomach?
3. The butterflies in the stomach of the runner on the left are in disarray, but they are aligned in the stomach of the runner on the right. What does this difference mean to you?

LIFE LESSON 39

Stress Is Good; Distress Is Bad

Stress is commonly discussed as something bad. When people say they are "so stressed," they usually mean they feel overwhelmed and defeated. But this feeling state is not *stress*; it's distress. The difference between these two person-states is the ***perception of control***.[47]

The first definition of stress in the *American Heritage Dictionary* is "importance, significance, or emphasis placed upon something."[48] When we are stressed, we are focused and motivated to make something happen. We are self-motivated if we perceive choice, competence, and community (Life Lessons 17, 18, & 19).

The person who proclaims, "I work best under pressure," understands the benefits of stress. Hans Selye, the Austrian-born founder of stress research, said: "Complete freedom from stress is death."[49]

Distress is the harmful feeling state. It is defined as "anxiety or suffering, severe strain resulting from exhaustion or an accident"[50] or "suffering of body or mind; pain, anguish; trouble, misfortune ... a condition of desperate need."[51]

We experience stress when our stressors are managed effectively; we are distressed when we are unprepared or ill-equipped to deal with a particular stressor. In other words, distress turns to stress when perceptions of personal control are increased. Anything that increases a feeling of *empowerment* (Life Lesson 25) should increase one's perception of personal control and reduce distress. Consider the following sequence of cognitive (self-talk) decisions accompanying the anticipation or the occurrence of an environmental event (e.g., an exam, a job talk, a performance responsibility, or a sporting event): a) You decide whether the event is important. If judged important, the event is a stressor; b) If the event is considered a stressor, you make a second cognitive appraisal: "Do I have personal control?"; c) If the answers to the three empowerment questions are "Yes," you experience motivating stress. Alternatively, if the appraisal of personal control is "No," the stressor results in debilitating distress.

Thinking Beyond the Illustration

Directions: Based on what you have read for this life lesson, respond to the questions below.

1. What can people do to get the "butterflies in their stomach" organized like the runner on the right?
2. Recall a time when you were nervous or on-edge about an upcoming event (e.g., an exam, a sports competition, or a public performance). Which runner in the illustration best reflects your motivational state at that time? Why?

77

Responding to the Illustration

Directions: Look at the illustration above. Refer to this illustration to answer the following questions.

1. What does this illustration mean to you?
2. Given the commonsense truth of this life lesson, is distress inevitable? Please explain.
3. What can an individual do to decrease the possibility of low personal control and distress?

LIFE LESSON 40

We Can't Control Everything

As reviewed in Life Lessons 25 and 39, anything that increases *empowerment* or perceived competence should increase a perception of personal control. Giving people more knowledge, resources, and interpersonal support should increase their personal control and prevent stress from becoming distress. However, personal control is a personal perception. It's in the eyes of the beholder.

Stephen Covey recommends we distinguish between our "Circle of Concern" and our "Circle of Influence," and focus our efforts on our domain of influence.[28] It's healthy to admit there are things we are concerned about but have little influence over—from the weather and politics to various management decisions that can affect our lives. Then, when negative consequences occur beyond our domain of influence, we do not experience distress because of a lack of personal control.

Sometimes events occur within our domain of influence, but we don't get distressed because we blame situational factors beyond our control. "I failed the exam because the teacher did not cover the material clearly, and many of the questions were unfair." As covered in Life Lesson 37, this misattribution is labeled the *self-serving bias*. While this bias protects our "self-esteem" and decreases the probability of experiencing distress, it can stifle attempts at personal improvement.

You can expand your domain of influence by setting goals that are *empowering* and **SMARTS**: "S" for *Specific* behaviors to perform; "M" for a *Motivational* connection to consequences to be gained from goal attainment; "A" for setting an *Attainable* stretch goal; "R" for a goal that is *Relevant* to a personal mission or ultimate vision; "T" for a goal that is *Trackable* for assessing progress; and "S" for *Share* your goal with others for social support and accountability.[52]

The "M" reflects *Motivational* rather than *Measurable* (a popular goal-setting M-word) because goal-setting should include an anticipation of a motivating consequence (i.e., outcome expectancy). The "T" for *Trackable* implies a *Measurable* process.

Thinking Beyond the Illustration

Directions: Based on what you have read for this life lesson, respond to the questions below.

1. Define a situation in which your level of perceived control is/was low. What factors or characteristics of this situation made/make you feel a low sense of personal control?
2. Define a recent situation at home, school, or work in which you attempted to maintain a sense of personal control and prevent stress from turning into distress? What did you say to yourself and/or do to make that happen?

Optimism Influences All Walks of Life.

Responding to the Illustration

Directions: Look at the illustration above. Refer to this illustration to answer the following questions.

1. In your opinion, what is the illustration attempting to demonstrate?
2. Why is the beggar experiencing more stress than distress?
3. Is the beggar a *success seeker* or a *failure avoider*? Please explain.

LIFE LESSON 41

Optimists Experience Less Distress

Optimism is reflected by the statement, "I expect the best." Optimistic people maintain the expectation that their life events, including personal actions, will turn out well. Most success seekers are optimistic, while failure avoiders are likely to be pessimists (Life Lesson 10).

Compared to pessimists, optimists maintain a sense of humor, perceive problems or challenges in a positive light, and plan for a successful future. They focus on what they can do—behavior—rather than on how they feel.[53] As a result, optimists handle their stressors constructively and thereby experience positive stress rather than negative distress.[54]

Optimists essentially expect to be successful at whatever they do. Hence they work harder than pessimists to reach their goals. Thus, optimists are beneficiaries of the *self-fulfilling prophecy*.[46] An optimistic perspective fuels a person's attempts to achieve more.

Question: Is optimism a **trait** (determined by nature) or a **state** (determined by nurture or a particular environmental context or set of circumstances)? The safest answer to this critical question: Both.

While a personality disposition predisposes individuals to be optimistic, pessimistic, or even cynical, the situation or context—especially behavioral consequences—certainly influence people to be more or less optimistic. Consider, for example, the overlap between feeling optimistic and feeling empowered (Life Lesson 25) and self-motivated (Life Lessons 17, 18, & 19). Anything that fuels these person-states enhances optimism.

More recently, scholars have distinguished between being *optimistic* (expecting the best) and being *hopeful* (working to achieve best expectations).[55] From this perspective, "I hope this happens," implies that "I can expect the best outcome if I do everything I know to do in order to achieve that outcome." Therefore, **hope** is the integration of *optimism* and *personal control*—indispensable person-states for experiencing beneficial stress rather than debilitating distress.

Thinking Beyond the Illustration

Directions: Based on what you have read for this life lesson, respond to the questions below.

1. Do you consider yourself to be generally an optimist or a pessimist or does this disposition depend on the situation? Please explain.
2. How might your answer to Question 1 influence your attitude, mindset, and behavior? For example, do you plan for negative consequences, as reflected by Murphy's Law: "Anything that can go wrong will"?

Responding to the Illustration

Directions: Look at the illustration above. Refer to this illustration to answer the following questions.

1. What does this illustration mean to you?
2. Do you know someone who appears to be a **Type A person** more than others? Please explain.
3. Do you know someone who seems to be the opposite of *Type A* most of the time (i.e., **Type B**)? Please explain.

LIFE LESSON 42

The Good and Bad of Type A

The illustration for this life lesson might seem familiar—perhaps too familiar. So many people have so much to do and not enough time to do it. Then personal goals are thwarted; personal control and optimism are diminished; and stress turns to distress. The result is often frustration, and frustration can lead to aggression and a demeanor that only increases distress. It's a vicious cycle that certainly decreases the propensity for a healthy mindset, beneficial relationships, and constructive work output.

People with a certain personality trait, referred to as *Type A*, are more likely to experience the time urgency and competitiveness depicted in the illustration. The initial research of the *Type A personality* associated this disposition with a higher risk for coronary disease,[56] but subsequent research indicated that Type A plus hostility (as depicted in the illustration) is the risk factor for a heart attack.[57] Thus, Type A individuals with an AC4P (actively-caring-for-people) mindset are not more prone to coronary disease.

A personality scale distinguishes between Type A *behavior* and Type A *emotion*,[58] with the Type A *emotion* putting people at risk for heart disease. For example, while you're rushing to save time (behavior), do you feel anger toward people who get in your way and slow you down (emotion)?

Type A-behavior individuals are likely goal-driven and self-motivated to get things done. They dislike wasting time and work hard to maintain personal control over life challenges they deem important. While these folks do experience more daily stressors than *Type B* individuals, a success-seeking and hopeful perspective leads to experiencing stress rather than distress.

On the negative side, Type A persons are more likely to experience frustration (Type A *emotion*), and this person-state can activate hostility and aggressive behavior. In addition, Type A folks often fail to appreciate the intrinsic value and flow of momentary pleasures, and they miss benefits from mindful meditation—relaxing inside and outside, and sensing the positive unique stimuli of the momentary present.

Thinking Beyond the Illustration

Directions: Based on what you have read for this life lesson, respond to the questions below.

1. To what extent does your life sometimes feel like a "Type A Behavior Zone"? Where and when do you feel this way?
2. Are you generally more Type A or Type B? To what extent does this categorization depend on the situation? Please explain.

Responding to the Illustration

Directions: Look at the illustration above. Refer to this illustration to answer the following questions.

1. What does the illustration mean to you?
2. Do you believe women in general are worse drivers than men? Why?
3. What other characteristics besides driving are ascribed to one gender versus the other? For example, are women more emotional and better caregivers than men, and do men make better corporate or political leaders than women? Please explain.

LIFE LESSON 43

Discrimination Is Good; Stereotyping Is Bad

Stereotyping occurs when people form an opinion about another person to some degree by that individual's relationship to a certain group. We tend to give global labels for people, such as student, patient, homosexual, athlete, or senior citizen. Each label activates a particular image and a set of characteristics. Then, the general label we give people influences how we view them, judge them, and react to their communication with us. The illustration for this life lesson reflects a gender stereotype that actually runs counter to statistics. As anyone who has purchased vehicle insurance knows, male drivers are more likely to experience a vehicle collision than female drivers.

Becoming more mindful of the vast differences between individuals and how these differences fluctuate as a function of time, place, and social context makes it difficult and irrational to attach general labels to people. Yet, let's face it, we do put people in categories. Such stereotyping is facilitated by best-selling books like *Men Are from Mars, Women Are from Venus*[59] and by popular personality tests like the Myers-Briggs Type Indicator[60] and the Primary Colors Inventory.[61]

Categorizing people and things is how we come to know, understand, and evaluate our surrounding environment. But, the key to reducing stereotyping and prejudice is to make *more* rather than fewer distinctions between people. When people pay more attention to the numerous differences among individuals and perceive how these differences vary across situations, it becomes increasingly difficult to put individuals in universal or generic categories.

Consider all the interpersonal conflict and violence that occurs because people can't handle diversity. They haven't been adequately socialized to appreciate and respect individual differences. Thus, discrimination per se is not wrong; it's a fact of living and learning. Just make more discriminations when evaluating and judging people. Personality labels pigeonhole people, including yourself, and limit possibilities. Situational awareness and interpersonal learning can overcome personal dispositions.

Thinking Beyond the Illustration

Directions: Based on what you have read for this life lesson, respond to the questions below.

1. Evaluating people with a global label (e.g., male, student, athlete, or homeless person) is called stereotyping. Is *stereotyping* good or bad? Please explain.
2. What stereotyping have you observed, either from personal experience or from observing others?

Responding to the Illustration

Directions: Look at the illustration above. Refer to this illustration to answer the following questions.

1. What does the illustration mean to you?
2. Why is communication with email, Twitter, Instagram, and other social media so popular?
3. What are the limitations (if any) of using email, a smartphone, or Twitter to communicate effectively with another person?

LIFE LESSON 44

The Power of Conversation

We start with a commonsense bottom line: Effective interpersonal conversation is paramount to cultivating a culture of empathy, compassion, and AC4P behavior.[62] The high-tech communication referenced in the illustration for this life lesson is not the answer, but rather we're talking about face-to-face communication.

Let's review the benefits of effective communication and thereby realize the "power of interpersonal conversation."

Resolving Interpersonal Conflict. Of course, an effective conversation can prevent or eliminate conflict. "Let's talk it out," as the saying goes.

Bringing Reality to Intangibles. What do these common terms mean: love, friendship, courage, loyalty, happiness, and forgiveness? We define another person's friendship, courage, or loyalty by talking about that individual in certain ways, both to ourselves and to others.

Defining Culture. It seems the *culture* of a group, school, sports team, company, community, or an entire country has become the most frequent explanation for good and bad outcomes arising from human interaction. In fact, a culture is defined by interpersonal conversations and the behaviors influenced by such communication.

Influencing Self-Esteem. How we talk to ourselves (intrapersonal conversation) both influences and reflects our *self-esteem*—our level of overall self-worth. In fact, our self-esteem goes up or down according to how we talk to ourselves about the way others talk about us (see Life Lesson 38).

Enabling Breakthroughs. Synergistic breakthroughs—going beyond business as usual and achieving more than expected—requires people to realize new possibilities, commit to going for more, and then make a concerted effort to overcome barriers. So how can we benefit from diversity, visualize possibilities, show commitment to go for a breakthrough, and identify barriers to overcome? You guessed it—through frank and open interpersonal and intrapersonal conversation.

Thinking Beyond the Illustration

Directions: Based on what you have read for this life lesson, respond to the questions below.

1. What are the beneficial consequences of effective interpersonal (one-to-one) conversation?
2. Have your words on email, Facebook, or Twitter ever been misunderstood or misinterpreted? Please explain.

Responding to the Illustration

Directions: Look at the illustration above. Refer to this illustration to answer the following questions.

1. How does the illustration show *empathy*—identifying with another person's situation, feelings, and motives?
2. How does the illustration reflect the Platinum Rule—"Treat others the way *they* want to be treated" (Life Lesson 27)?
3. What are the advantages of the Platinum Rule over the more common Golden Rule—"Treat others the way *you* want to be treated"?

LIFE LESSON 45

The Power of Empathy

Whether the topic is *empathic listening*, empathic leadership, or empathic feedback, the focus is on the other person's feelings, needs, or perceptions. It's more than the *Golden Rule*: "Treat others as *you* would like to be treated." As covered in Life Lesson 27, it's the *Platinum Rule*: "Treat others as *they* want to be treated."[29]

We sympathize when we express concern or understanding for another individual's situation, but we empathize when we identify with another person's situation and realize what it's like to be in the other person's shoes. Let's consider some basic strategies for achieving an empathic level of appreciation.

Take off your blinders. Minimize the reactive filters (or *premature cognitive commitment*, Life Lesson 34) that bias interpersonal communication.

Ask more questions. This is how you truly understand the other person's position, diagnose the problem, and design an optimal AC4P intervention plan. Recall the *nondirective* stance advised when giving corrective feedback (Life Lesson 8).

Listen for more than words. Not only must we hear every word in a conversation, we must be sensitive to feelings, passion, and commitment—reflected by the individual's expressive body language.

Use your imagination. When you observe another person's less-than-optimal behavior, try to view the situation from that individual's perspective. Imagine what defense mechanisms *you* might use to protect *your* ego or self-esteem (Life Lesson 8).

Weigh alternatives. When considering action plans for improvement, try to view various alternatives by putting yourself in the same shoes as the other person. Derive an action plan you would be willing to follow. You do this by bringing empathy to your interpersonal conversations. With more empathy, more compassion is energized, and then more benefits result from an AC4P plan that takes into account the perspectives and circumstances of those served by the intervention.

Thinking Beyond the Illustration

Directions: Based on what you have read for this life lesson, respond to the questions below.

1. What holds people back from practicing the Platinum Rule?
2. Recall and define two situations: a) one in which your perspective was seriously considered and b) another situation when it was not.

Responding to the Illustration

Directions: Look at the illustration above. Refer to this illustration to answer the following questions.

1. What message is depicted in the illustration?
2. How important is *interpersonal trust* among peers, and between children and their parents, students and their teachers, employees and their supervisors? Please explain.
3. From your experience, what are some ways to build trust between individuals?

LIFE LESSON 46

Build Interpersonal Trust

Effective parents, teachers, coaches, and supervisors are trustworthy, and they engender trust among others. What does this mean? You could be confident a person means well, but you might doubt his or her ability to complete the intended task. In this case, you trust the individual's intentions, but you lack confidence in the capability of this person to make good on his or her promises. "She is well intended, but she doesn't have what it takes to make it happen."

In contrast, people can have faith in the ability of others, but mistrust these individuals' intentions. The followers might believe their leader has the intellect and skills to make a difference, but they're not sure their welfare is considered in this person's decision-making. "He has the talent and support system to make it happen, but he's looking out for his own best interests more than ours."

The following seven C-words reflect strategies for building *interpersonal trust* in a person's intention and ability: *Communication*, *Caring*, *Candor*, *Consistency*, *Commitment*, *Consensus*, and *Character*.[63]

The trust-building value of these C's is reflected by their definitions and common usage. In fact, Communication, Caring, Consistency, Consensus, and Commitment are each addressed in prior life lessons. The second definition of Candor, besides being frank and open, is "freedom from prejudice or stereotyping."[64] When a person's communication reflects a stereotype (Life Lesson 43), there's mistrust.

With regard to *Character* and trust-building, consider that people with character are honest, ethical, principled, and worthy of another person's trust. They have the courage to admit their mistakes with a sincere apology and a request for forgiveness. Plus, these trustworthy individuals avoid talking about deficiencies in others. They realize that publicly criticizing or demeaning other individuals leads to interpersonal suspicion and mistrust; therefore, they commit to a policy of "No back-stabbing." They always talk about other people as if those other people can hear them.

Thinking Beyond the Illustration

Directions: Based on what you have read for this life lesson, respond to the questions below.

1. Consider an individual you trust, and offer some reasons you trust him or her.
2. Consider an individual you do not trust, and offer a rationale for your selection.

Responding to the Illustration

Directions: Look at the illustration above. Refer to this illustration to answer the following questions.

1. How does the illustration reflect the three words of this life lesson?
2. When will the campers experience maximum fear—the adrenaline rush—from the bear?
3. What is the relevance of this life lesson for controlling or improving our emotions?

LIFE LESSON 47

Behavior Precedes Emotion

Think of an *emotion*—fear, sadness, anger, happiness, disgust, or surprise. Do these emotions drive behavior? Do we cry because we are sad, lash out because we are angry, and tremble because we are afraid?

Does a person experience fear and then respond accordingly, depending on the situation? The illustration for this life lesson suggests the opposite. The camper is calm, cool, and collected as he prepares to run from the bear. Soon he will be running to escape the bear and then he will experience the emotion of fear.

Indeed, contrary to common sense our body reacts first to an external stimulus—a triggering event—with accelerated heart rate, perspiration, and trembling. Then our brain's cortex interprets our bodily responses as a particular emotion, depending on the situation.[65] We are afraid because we tremble; we feel sad because we cry; angry because we lash out; and we're happy because we're smiling.

Thus, we act ourselves into a particular emotion. Note the connection of this life lesson to the *Consistency Principle* (Life Lessons 30 & 31), and the evidence-based conclusion that effective behavioral therapy acts a client into related thinking.

The *facial feedback technique* advocated by positive-psychology researchers connects directly to this life lesson. Specifically, research has demonstrated that people who are manipulated into a smiling expression actually feel happier.[66] Just activating one smiling muscle by holding a pencil in your teeth can make you feel a little better. But a hearty smile that raises your cheeks and crinkles your eyes will do even more to raise your spirits.[67] The opposite is also true. Put on an angry face and you'll feel angrier. Your facial expressions do more than display your feelings; they feed your feelings.

Conclusion: Put on a happy face and talk as if you are optimistic, in control, and self-motivated and you will likely act yourself into a happier state of mind. You can do the same for others: Inspire people to perform AC4P behavior and you will inspire a positive emotion in them.

Thinking Beyond the Illustration

Directions: Based on what you have read for this life lesson, respond to the questions below.

1. Explain the connection between this life lesson and a phrase used by some clinical psychologists, "We can act people into a new way of thinking."
2. Recall an emotional experience (positive or negative) and explain whether that event supports or does not support this life lesson.

93

Responding to the Illustration

Directions: Look at the illustration above. Refer to this illustration to answer the following questions.

1. What is the point of this illustration?
2. Can you connect the illustration to real-world perceptions and/or experiences of humans? Please explain.
3. Have you ever thought that the victim of an unfortunate event deserved it?

LIFE LESSON 48

Justice Is a Matter of Perception

It's common for people to believe that victims of crimes or "accidents" caused their own fate. Social psychologists call this phenomenon the *just-world hypothesis*—we get what we deserve and we deserve what we get.[68]

Consider how the belief in a just world can be a barrier to helping others. Here we have another attributional bias (Life Lessons 35, 36, & 37). When deriving an explanation for an unfortunate incident, observers influenced by the just-world hypothesis might blame the victim(s). Such bias provides a convenient excuse for not helping someone.

Have you ever observed someone performing risky behavior and said to yourself something like, "What a dumb thing to do; if he gets hurt he deserves it"? Social psychologists assume this thinking is a form of self-defense that helps us maintain a belief that life is safe, orderly, and predictable.[69] If life were unfair and random, innocent people like ourselves could also be victimized and injured.

Since most people see themselves as decent and basically good, bad things won't happen to them. These folks see themselves as the largest fish in the illustration for this life lesson. Note how this attributional defense mechanism influences the familiar self-talk of risk takers, "It won't happen to me. It happens to the other guy." We've all been there, right? We take a chance—a calculated risk—because we think we're safe and secure in a just world.

Consider that those who suffer injuries also believed in a "just world." They didn't expect anything bad to happen to them—only to the other guy. Perhaps the *just-world hypothesis* should be interpreted as "We need to do everything we know to do to protect each other from potential harm in order to make our world fair to as many of the other guys as possible."

It is certainly *not* a just world, but as more AC4P behavior occurs worldwide, human well-being and life satisfaction will increase successively and the world will seem more fair to more people.

Thinking Beyond the Illustration

Directions: Based on what you have read for this life lesson, respond to the questions below.

1. To what extent do you believe the common statement, "Everything happens for a reason"? Please explain.
2. What are potential advantages and/or disadvantages in believing that everything happens for a reason?

Responding to the Illustration

Directions: Look at the illustration above. Refer to this illustration to answer the following questions.

1. Why are the children in the illustration laughing?
2. Why might these children react differently the next time they experience a similar situation with a police officer?
3. Was the driver a *success seeker* or a *failure avoider* when he pulled over (Life Lesson 10)? Please explain.

We Learn Every Day in Three Ways

The illustration for this life lesson depicts three types of learning we usually experience every day: *classical conditioning, operant conditioning*, and *observational learning*.

We have already covered two of these learning paradigms in prior life lessons. Specifically, Life Lessons 2, 3, and 4 explained how our behavior is influenced by positive and negative consequences. This is *operant conditioning*.

Recall the ABC Model in Life Lesson 3. When an **A**ctivator informs us of a certain **C**onsequence following a particular **B**ehavior, it's an incentive or a disincentive. We choose to perform that behavior in order to receive a positive consequence or avoid a negative consequence. In our illustration, flashing blue lights signaled the driver to pull over, and he chose to do so in order to avoid a consequence more negative than a traffic ticket.

The siblings in the back seat are happy, "Oh boy, here comes a nice police officer with a gun to give us some special attention." However, through observational learning (Life Lessons 13 & 14), these kids will soon learn from the body language and verbal behavior of their parents that this is not a pleasant experience.

The third learning paradigm reflected in the illustration is *classical conditioning*. This has not been explicitly covered in a prior life lesson, although this learning process was implied wherever an emotional reaction was suggested by an illustration (e.g., the stress or distress experiences of the runners in Life Lesson 39 and the Type A emotions depicted in the illustration for Life Lesson 42).

The negative reaction to a flashing blue light on a police car is not voluntary; rather the blue light causes an involuntary automatic nervous-system response. This negative reaction is not experienced by the children in the illustration because they have not yet learned about the aversive consequences of the blue light—referred to as a **conditioned stimulus** because this stimulus-response association is learned.

Thinking Beyond the Illustration

Directions: Based on what you have read for this life lesson, respond to the questions below.

1. Did the flashing blue light of the police car in the illustration cause an emotional reaction from the driver? Please explain.
2. Please define a stimulus or an environmental event that causes an emotional reaction from you (positive or negative), but also provides behavioral direction.

Responding to the Illustration

Directions: Look at the illustration above. Refer to this illustration to answer the following questions.

1. What does this illustration mean to you?
2. Do you believe the slogan, "You can't teach an old dog new tricks"? Please explain.
3. What does the title of this life lesson mean to you?

The Legacy of Teaching and Learning

Congratulations! You are now learning the last of 50 research-based life lessons and related applications for enhancing human well-being. I sincerely hope you have acquired more than an *understanding* of these select life lessons from psychological science. I hope you *believe* in the validity of the evidence-based life lessons presented here to benefit interpersonal behaviors, perceptions, and attitudes, and will want to *teach* some of these to others.

"We live, we love, we learn, and we leave a legacy." This profound quotation from Stephen R. Covey says it all.[28] Consider the remarkable legacy of teaching and learning. When people—our children, students, friends, and colleagues—learn from our teaching, they might not only apply the principles and procedures we teach, they might pass them on. In turn, they leave their own teaching/learning legacy.

Let's consider connections between Stephen Covey's quotation and Abraham Maslow's Hierarchy of Needs.[70] At the bottom we have the "to live" physiological needs. Next, we have the "to love" and "to learn" needs for social acceptance, self-esteem, and *self-actualization*. At the top of Maslow's Hierarchy is *self-transcendence*—the need to go beyond our own needs to benefit someone else's well-being. We call this "actively caring for people"—www.ac4p.org.

The connection between these need hierarchies, proposed by two of the most provocative thought leaders of the 20th century is obvious, right? Maslow claimed the best we can be is to go beyond ourselves for others; Covey challenged us to leave a legacy of which we would be proud. Covey and Maslow have defined an enviable daily mission and long-term vision for us all.

Practice the life lessons from this LifeCOACH manual to enhance the well-being of others and you will exemplify *self-transcendence*. Teach others what you learn from applying these life lessons and you will leave a positive teaching/learning legacy of which you can be extremely proud. You will enrich your own life by actively caring for the lives of others.

Thinking Beyond the Illustration

Directions: Based on what you have read for this life lesson, respond to the questions below.

1. What holds people back from continuously learning, including being open to receiving corrective feedback from others?
2. Which of the 50 life lessons in this teaching/learning manual will you share with or teach others? Please explain why.

GLOSSARY OF KEY TERMS

ABC (activator-behavior-consequence): the three-term contingency of applied behavioral science (ABS), specifying that a stimulus event (an activator) occurring before a behavior provides direction (e.g., an incentive or a disincentive), whereas the consequence following a behavior provides motivation for repeating the preceding behavior.

Activator: an environmental event (e.g., directions from a sign or a person, an incentive or disincentive) implemented to influence the occurrence of a particular target behavior.

Actively Caring for People (AC4P): the application of behavioral science and select principles from humanism to increase the frequency and improve the quality of behavior that benefits human health, safety, security, and/or welfare—referred to as humanistic behaviorism.

AC4P Coaching: interpersonal communication whereby one individual (the teacher, coach, or parent) employs principles of humanistic behaviorism in order to benefit the observed behavior of another individual (the learner).

AC4P Culture: an environmental context or setting (e.g., a workplace, school, or home) where people interact daily on behalf of the health, safety, security, and well-being of everyone else in the surroundings with a spirit of win/win interdependence and self-transcendence.

Applied Behavioral Science (ABS): the application of research-based principles derived from experimental behavior analysis to increase the occurrence of desirable behaviors and decrease the frequency of undesirable behaviors.

Attributional Bias: a prejudiced assumption of why a person is acting in a certain way—reactive thinking as opposed to reflective thinking.

Authority Principle: the tendency to comply with a request from a person with presumed credibility and perhaps influence over relevant behavioral consequences.

Behavior-Based Feedback: interpersonal communication following the occurrence of an observed behavior that shows the performer what s/he did correctly (supportive feedback) and/or incorrectly (corrective feedback).

Behavior-Based Safety (BBS): the systematic application of applied behavioral science (ABS) to prevent personal injury by increasing the occurrence of safe behavior and decreasing the frequency of at-risk (or unsafe) behavior, typically manifested by a peer-to-peer behavioral observation-and-feedback process.

Bystander Effect: the tendency for any given observer of a person needing help to be less likely to give aid if other bystanders are present, presumably due to diffusion of personal responsibility.

Choice: the perception of having more than one option with regard to accomplishing a particular task or action plan.

Classical Conditioning: a learning process whereby a previously neutral stimulus comes to elicit (or cause) an automatic or reactive response (or behavior)—an involuntary conditioned response.

Cognitive Dissonance: tension or discomfort experienced when an individual's behavior is inconsistent with his/her attitude, belief, and/or values, or vice versa.

Community: the perception of relatedness or belongingness with others, and often an experience of interdependent social or group support regarding the accomplishment of a certain challenge or assignment.

Compassion: AC4P action or behavior following empathy—a sincere concern for another person's welfare or well-being.

Competence: the perception or belief that an individual has the knowledge, skill, and ability to accomplish a certain task effectively.

Conditioned Stimulus: a stimulus previously neutral with regard to triggering a particular response acquires the capacity to elicit that same response (a conditioned response) through the learning process of classical conditioning.

Consequence: an environmental event (positive or negative) that naturally occurs (i.e., intrinsic) after a behavior or is added to the situation (i.e., extrinsic) in order to influence a certain behavior, which may or may not influence the frequency or improve the quality of the preceding behavior.

Consistency: the pressure to behave in ways that are in concert with our attitudes, beliefs, or values; or to behave in ways others expect us to behave.

Contingency Management: manipulating an activator and the consequence(s) of a target behavior in order to increase (with an incentive/reward) or decrease (with a disincentive/penalty) its quality or its frequency of occurrence.

Corrective Feedback: behavior-focused information given to an individual after s/he performs an undesirable or less-than-optimal behavior, often manifested in a one-to-one coaching interaction.

Descriptive Norm: the commonly observed or reported behavior of other people.

Disincentive: an activator (or extrinsic stimulus) that announces the delivery of a certain negative consequence (a penalty) following the occurrence of a designated unwanted behavior.

Disposition: an internal trait or person-state of an individual that predisposes or influences his/her behavior at a certain time and place.

Distress: the physiological and psychological reaction to an event that is perceived as important—a stressor—but appraised as threatening or overwhelming and beyond the person's current domain of personal control.

Door-in-the-Face Technique: making a large, irrational, behavioral request in order to make a subsequent smaller request seem much more reasonable and doable.

Education: teaching one or more individuals awareness, theory, or procedures related to a certain task or the circumstances related to that task.

Emotion: a potent and potentially long-term reaction to a person or a situation that can motivate relevant self-directed behavior.

Emotional Intelligence: one's ability to a) remain in control and optimistic following personal failure and frustration, b) understand and empathize with other people and work with them cooperatively, and c) give up a soon, certain, and positive consequence for a delayed and uncertain but larger positive consequence.

Empathic Listening: the highest level of interpersonal listening whereby the listener attempts to identify with and understand the speaker's feelings, attitude, motives, and behavior, as well as the circumstances influencing relevant dispositions and behavior.

Empathy: attempting to identify with and understand another individual's circumstances that influence his/her feelings, attitude, motives, and behavior.

Empowerment: an individual's belief or confidence that s/he can master a particular assignment or accomplish a certain task, determined by answering "Yes" to three questions—Can I do it? Will it work? and Is it worth it?

Extrinsic: a stimulus event external to the individual, considered to be an activator or a consequence when applied to influence (or motivate) the occurrence of a target behavior.

Extrinsic Motivator: an activator (e.g., an incentive or disincentive) that influences the occurrence of a behavior in order to gain a positive consequence, avoid a negative consequence, or escape an aversive environmental event.

Extrinsic Reward: a positive behavioral consequence delivered after the occurrence or outcome of behavior(s) in order to support the behavior(s) and/or to enhance an individual's sense of competence or self-efficacy.

Extrinsic Stimulus: an observable and external environmental event that might direct behavior (as an activator) or motivate behavior (as a positive or negative consequence).

Facial-Feedback Technique: manipulating one's facial muscles (e.g., force a smile) to trigger a corresponding emotion (e.g., happiness or positive affect).

Failure Avoider: an individual performing a certain behavior in order to avoid a negative consequence.

Feedback: behavior-focused information (supportive or corrective) following the performance of a behavior, delivered to influence the frequency and/or the quality of the preceding behavior.

Foot-in-the-Door Technique: soliciting a small behavioral commitment for a person to perform a relatively convenient behavior in order to obtain subsequent compliance with a more inconvenient behavior with greater response cost.

Fundamental Attribution Error: the tendency for an observer of another person's behavior to underestimate the impact of the context (situational factors) and overestimate the impact of dispositional factors (person-states and/or traits).

Groupthink: the tendency for group members to agree, resulting in conformity from individuals within that group who may hold a different view.

Hope: the combination of optimism and personal control, contributing to the belief that positive expectations will eventuate if relevant behaviors are performed.

Humanism: an appreciation of empathy, diversity, and human dignity; a sincere concern for human well-being.

Humanistic Behaviorism: making applications of applied behavioral science (ABS), implemented to improve human performance, more effective by practicing empathy and considering such person-states as self-esteem, self-efficacy, belongingness, personal control, and optimism.

Hypocrisy Effect: the occurrence of a desired target behavior is motivated by activating a "guilt trip"—participants perceive an inconsistency between their current personal commitment to perform a certain desirable behavior and their lack of previously performing that behavior (i.e., they realize an inconsistency between their prior behavior and a current behavioral commitment).

If-Then Contingency: an incentive or disincentive whereby an activator announces the delivery of a reward or a penalty following the occurrence of a desired or undesired behavior, respectively.

Incentive: an announcement (an activator) that specifies the availability of a positive consequence (a reward) following the performance of a designated behavior or a desirable outcome of more than one behavior.

Independence: an individualistic viewpoint or mindset that sets the occasion for self-focused behavior ("I can do this myself") and inhibits other-focused behavior ("Let's work together to make this happen").

Injunctive Norm: the desirable behavior in a particular situation or what one "ought to do."

Interdependence: a collectivistic, we-need-each-other viewpoint or mindset that facilitates and supports AC4P behavior—acts performed on behalf of the health, safety, security, and/or well-being of others.

Interpersonal Trust: the AC4P connection between people that enables the cultivation of an AC4P culture with the seven C's—communication, caring, candor, consistency, commitment, consensus, and character—along with the interpersonal behavior-based feedback tools provided in this LifeCOACH manual.

Intrinsic Consequence: a positive or negative stimulus event that flows naturally after a behavior and keeps it going (a positive reinforcer) or causes it to decrease in frequency or stop completely (a punisher).

Just-World Hypothesis: the belief that the world is fair (or just) and that people therefore get what they deserve and deserve what they get.

Leadership: inspiring people to be self-motivated and feel empowered to perform one or more goal-directed behaviors (i.e., discretionary behavior).

Management: motivating one or more behaviors to occur through an external or extrinsic accountability system (e.g., activator, behavioral feedback, incentive, disincentive, rule, mandate, interpersonal recognition, or reprimand).

Nondirective Stance: practicing empathic listening to learn another person's perceptions and relevant circumstances before providing advice or direction.

Now-That Reward: a positive behavioral consequence (e.g., behavior-based recognition or supportive feedback) delivered after observing the occurrence of a desirable behavior—given to express sincere appreciation for the behavior and to potentially influence the recipient's perceived competence and self-motivation, as well as to increase the probability that the desired behavior will reoccur.

Observational Learning: initiating or improving the performance of one or more behaviors by watching one or more individuals perform the behavior(s).

Operant Conditioning: voluntary behavior comes to be controlled by a consequence following its occurrence.

Optimism: the expectation that the consequences of one or more behaviors will be positive—a challenge will be handled successfully.

Outcome Expectancy: anticipating the positive consequence(s) to follow the occurrence of one or more goal-directed behaviors and believing that achieving the consequence is worth the effort and time involved—the response cost.

Penalty: a negative consequence following a designated behavior or an outcome of one or more behaviors that may or may not influence recurrence of the behavior(s).

Perception of Control: an individual believes s/he has personal influence over the environmental factors that determine successful performance of one or more behaviors in order to achieve a desired consequence or avoid an aversive consequence.

Performance: the output or outcome of a process or system which includes input from behavior, dispositions (person-states and traits), and situational factors.

Personal Control: one's perception of having the ability or competence to accomplish a particular task successfully—feeling empowered to meet a challenge.

Person-State: a personal disposition (e.g., expectancy, attitude, or personality characteristic) that influences an individual's behavior but varies as a function of the situation or environmental context.

Premature Cognitive Commitment: the notion that people often hold on stubbornly to a preconceived perception about someone or something (i.e., inflexible prejudice) as the result of prior personal experience, attitudes, cognitions, and/or behaviors.

Principle of Conformity: a researched-based social norm reflecting the tendency for people to adjust their behavior or decision-making to coincide with a group standard or their observations of others' similar behavior.

Principle of Consistency: the research-based dynamic that people alter their attitudes, beliefs, and/or perceptions to be consistent with their behavior, and vice versa.

Reciprocity Principle: the social norm that obligates people to repay others with the form of behavior (positive or negative) they had previously received from them—"pay-it-forward" or "pay back."

Reinforcer: an extrinsic (extra) or intrinsic (natural) stimulus or environmental event that increases the frequency and/or the form of the behavior it follows.

Response-Efficacy: an individual's belief or confidence that performing one or more goal-directed behaviors will contribute to achieving a desired outcome, mission, or long-term vision.

Reward: a positive consequence following a designated behavior or an outcome of more than one behavior that may or may not influence recurrence of the behavior(s).

Selection by Consequences: one of B.F. Skinner's legacies that reflects the motivational principle that people do what they do to gain a positive consequence or to avoid or escape a negative consequence.

Selective Perception: the process of interpreting and organizing sensory information that is biased by prior experience and/or expectations and may influence attitude, thinking, and behavior.

Self-Accountability: internal motivation (from within an individual) to perform one or more self-directed behaviors.

Self-Actualization: the top of Maslow's *initial* Hierarchy of Needs at which a person feels a sense of ultimate achievement—having fulfilled one's potential.

Self-Directed Behavior: self-motivated behavior that is not solely motivated by an external or extrinsic motivator (e.g., an incentive or a disincentive).

Self-Efficacy: an individual's belief or confidence that s/he has the knowledge, skill, and ability to perform the goal-directed behaviors needed to accomplish a certain task.

Self-Esteem: a general or overall feeling of self-worth that influences one's propensity to perform AC4P behavior.

Self-Fulfilling Prophecy: a prediction or expectation that directly or indirectly causes itself to become true because relevant behavior is influenced to confirm the prophecy.

Self-Motivation: a person-state that reflects internal drive to perform a certain behavior or achieve a particular outcome of one or more behaviors from a self-directed and self-accountability perspective.

Self-Persuasion: internal cognitive direction following a behavior-focused intervention that encourages personal buy-in and commitment.

Self-Serving Bias: taking personal credit for our successes, but blaming our failures on situational factors in order to protect our self-esteem and maintain a positive view of ourselves.

Self-Talk: interpersonal conversation (or covert behavior) that can influence overt behavior and often reflects and/or affects one's attitude, perception, self-esteem, and/or self-motivation.

Self-Transcendence: the top of Maslow's *revised* Hierarchy of Needs whereby an AC4P mindset is realized, and the individual experiences personal fulfillment and positive reinforcement when performing AC4P behavior—behavior contributing to the health, safety, security, or well-being of one or more persons.

SMARTS Goal: a behavior-focused objective defined by making it **S**pecific, **M**otivational, **A**ttainable, **R**elevant, **T**rackable, and **S**hared.

Social Label: a positive or negative attribute given overtly to an individual which influences that individual to perform behavior consistent with that label.

Social Proof: the tendency to look to others for guidance on what behaviors are appropriate or inappropriate in a particular situation, especially in an unfamiliar setting.

State: a disposition to feel and/or act in a particular way as the result of current life circumstances and/or environmental conditions.

Stereotyping: assuming (or pre-judging) that members of a particular group share certain characteristics or behaviors.

Stress: the physiological and psychological reaction to an event perceived as important and challenging—a stressor—and appraised as within one's current domain of personal control.

Success Seeker: an individual performing one or more behaviors in order to earn a positive consequence, which can be intrinsic or extrinsic.

Supportive Feedback: a now-that reward (or positive recognition) delivered after observing an individual's desirable behavior, which is most rewarding and influential when it can SOAR—it is *Specific* (designates the behavior); *On time* (occurs soon after the behavior is observed); *Appropriate* for the knowledge, ability, and experience of the performer; and shows *Real* appreciation for the individual's competence and effort.

Synergy: a process of interdependent participation in a goal-directed activity that results in greater achievement than possible from all participants performing alone and independently.

Systems Thinking: a perspective of win/win, interdependency, teamwork, and synergy that optimizes an organizational, educational, or family system; realizing that the consequence for one behavior can serve as the activator for the next behavior, leading to a spiral causality of AC4P-focused synergism initiated by one AC4P behavior and the Principles of Reciprocity and Consistency.

Training: providing behavior-focused direction and feedback regarding the quality of one or more specified behaviors performed to achieve a designated outcome.

Trait: a disposition to feel and act in a particular way, presumed to be a stable life-long personality characteristic resulting from nature rather than nurture.

Type A Personality: a disposition (or person-trait) reflecting people who are competitive, ambitious, hard-driving, impatient, aggressive, and anger-prone.

Type B Personality: a disposition (or person-trait) reflecting people who are easygoing, relaxed, and laid back—capable of living in the present and enjoying the moment.

Vicarious Punishment: observational learning whereby the negative consequence given to one or more persons following undesirable behavior influences an observer of this interaction to decrease the occurrence of that behavior.

Vicarious Reciprocity: AC4P behavior is facilitated when an individual observes or learns about the pay-it-forward AC4P behavior of one or more other persons who were influenced by the Principle of Reciprocity.

Vicarious Reinforcement: observational learning whereby the positive consequence given to one or more persons following a desirable behavior influences an observer of that interaction to increase the frequency or improve the quality of his/her performance of that behavior.

Vision: a distant or ultimate objective or aspiration, presumed to be reached or achieved through ongoing SMARTS goal-setting and the successive achievement of the relevant SMARTS goals.

REFERENCE NOTES

1. Skinner, B. F. (1938). *The behavior of organisms: An experimental analysis.* Acton, MA: Copley; Skinner, B. F. (1953). *Science and human behavior.* New York: Macmillan; Skinner, B. F. (1974). *About behaviorism.* New York: Alfred A. Knopf.

2. Geller, E. S. (2001). *The psychology of safety handbook.* Boca Raton, FL: CRC Press; McSween, T. S. (2003). *The values-based safety process: Improving your safety culture with a behavioral approach* (2nd ed.). New York: Van Nostrand Reinhold; Sulzer-Azaroff, B., & Austin, J. (2000). Does BBS Work? Behavior-based safety and injury reduction: A survey of the evidence. *Professional Safety, 45,* 19–24.

3. Premack, D. (1959). Toward empirical behavior laws: 1. Positive reinforcement. *Psychological Review, 66*(4), 219–233.

4. Kohn, A. (1993). *Punished by rewards: The trouble with gold stars, incentive plans, A's, praise, and other bribes.* Boston: Houghton Mifflin.

5. Cameron, J., & Pierce, W. D. (1994). Reinforcement, reward, and intrinsic motivation: A meta-analysis. *Review of Educational Research, 65*(3), 363–423; Eisenberger, R., & Cameron, J. (1996). Detrimental effects of reward: Reality or myth? *American Psychologist, 51*(11), 1153–1166.

6. Goleman, D. (1995). *Emotional intelligence.* New York: Bantam Books; Goleman, D. (1998). *Working with emotional intelligence.* New York: Bantam Books.

7. Mischel, W. (2014). *The marshmallow test: Mastering self-control.* New York: Little, Brown.

8. Shoda, Y., Mischel, W., & Peake, P. K. (1990). Predicting adolescent cognitive and self-regulatory competition from preschool delay of gratification. *Developmental Psychology, 26,* 978–997.

9. Chance, P. (2008). *The teacher's craft: The 10 essential skills of effective teaching.* Long Grove, IL: Waveland Press, Inc.; Reed, D. et al. (2016). Actively caring for higher education. In E.S. Geller (Ed.), *Applied psychology: Actively caring for people* (pp. 563–593). New York: Cambridge University Press; Thorndike, E. L. (1931). *Human learning.* Cambridge, MA: MIT Press.

10. Carnegie, D. (1936). *How to win friends and influence people* (1981 ed.). New York: Galahad Books.

11. Bandura, A. (1982). Self-efficacy mechanism in human agency. *American Psychologist, 37,* 122–147; Bandura, A. (1997). *Self-efficacy: The exercise of control.* New York: Freeman.

12. Covington, M. V. (1992). *Making the grade: A self-worth perspective on motivation and school reform.* New York: Cambridge University Press; Martin, A. J., & Marsh, H. W. (2003). Fear of failure: Friend or foe? *Australian Psychologist, 38,* 31–38.

13. Covington, M. V., & Roberts, B. W. (1994). Self-worth and college achievement: Motivational and personality correlates. In P. R. Pintrich, D. R. Brown, & C. E. Weinstein (Eds.), *Student motivation, cognition, and learning: Essays in honor of Wilbert J. McKeachie.* Hillsdale, NJ: Earlbaum.

14. Bandura, A. (1969). *Principles of behavior modification.* New York: Holt, Reinhold, & Winston.

15. Cialdini, R. B. (2001). *Influence: Science and practice* (6th ed.). Boston: Pearson.

16. Cialdini, R. B., Kallgren, C. A., & Reno, R. R. (1991). A focus theory of normative conduct: A theoretical refinement and reevaluation of the role of norms in human behavior. *Advances in Experimental Social Psychology, 24,* 201–234.

17. Goldstein, N. J., Cialdini, R. B., & Griskevicius, V. (2008). A room with a viewpoint: Using social norms to motivate environmental conservation in hotels. *Journal of Consumer Research, 35*(3), 472–482.

18. Geller, E. S. (2016). The psychology of self-motivation. In E. S. Geller (Ed.), *Applied psychology: Actively caring for people* (pp. 83–118). New York: Cambridge University Press.

19. Smith, R. C., & Geller, E. S. (2016). Actively caring to prevent alcohol abuse. In E. S. Geller (Ed.), *Applied psychology: Actively caring for people* (pp. 396–419). New York: Cambridge University Press.

20. Chance, P. (2008). *The teacher's craft: The 10 essential skills of effective teaching.* Long Grove, IL: Waveland Press.

21. Deci, E. L. (1975). *Intrinsic motivation.* New York: Plenum; Deci, E. L., & Flaste, R. (1995). *Why we do what we do: Understanding self-motivation.* New York: Penguin Books; Deci, E. L., & Ryan, R. M. (1995). *Intrinsic motivation and self-determinism in human behavior.* New York: Plenum; Ryan, R. M., & Deci, E. L. (2000). Self-determinism theory and the foundation of intrinsic motivation, social development, and well-being. *American Psychologist, 55,* 68–75; Geller, E. S. (2016). The psychology of self-motivation. In E. S. Geller (Ed.), *Applied psychology: Actively caring for people* (pp. 83–118). New York: Cambridge University Press.

22. Chance, P. (2008). *The teacher's craft: The 10 essential skills of effective teaching* (p. 95). Long Grove, IL: Waveland Press.

23. Deci, E. L., & Flaste, R. (1995). *Why we do what we do: Understanding self-motivation.* New York: Penguin Books.

24. Latane, B., & Darley, J. M. (1968). Group inhibition of bystander intervention. *Journal of Personality and Social Psychology, 10,* 215–221; Latane, B., & Darley, J. M. (1970). *The unresponsive bystander: Why doesn't he help?* New York: Appleton-Century-Crofts.

25. Deming, W. E. (1991, May). *Quality, productivity, and competitive position.* Four-day workshop presented in Cincinnati, Ohio, by Quality Enhancement Seminars, Inc., Los Angeles, CA.

26. Deming, W. E. (1986). *Out of the crisis.* Cambridge, MA: Massachusetts Institute of Technology, Center for Advanced Engineering Study; Deming, W. E. (1993). *The new economics for industry, government, and education.* Cambridge, MA: Massachusetts Institute of Technology, Center for Advanced Engineering Study.

27. Geller, E. S. (2016). The psychology of AC4P behavior. In E. S. Geller (Ed.), *Applied psychology: Actively caring for people* (pp. 45–82). New York: Cambridge University Press.

28. Covey, S. R. (1989). *The seven habits of highly effective people: Restoring the character ethic.* New York: Simon and Schuster.

29. Alessandra, T., & O'Connor, M. S. (1998). *The platinum rule: Discover the four business personalities and how they can lead you to success.* New York: Warner Business Books.

30. Cialdini, R. B., Vincent, J. E., Lewis, S. K., Catalan, J., Wheeler, D., & Darby, B. L. (1975). Reciprocal concessions procedure for inducing compliance: The door-in-the-face technique. *Journal of Personality and Social Psychology, 31,* 206–215.

31. Schwartzvald, D., Raz, M., & Zwibel, M. (1979). The applicability of the door-in-the-face technique when established behavioral customs exist. *Journal of Applied Social Psychology, 9,* 576–586.

32. Festinger, L. (1957). *A theory of cognitive dissonance.* Stanford, CA: Stanford University Press.

33. Bem, D. J. (1972). Self-perception theory. In L. Berkowitz (Ed.), *Advances in experimental psychology* (Vol. 6) (pp. 1–62). New York: Academic Press.

34. Freedman, J. L., & Fraser, S. C. (1966). Compliance without pressure: The foot-in-the-door technique. *Journal of Personality and Social Psychology, 4,* 195–202.

35. Cialdini, R. B., Eisenberg, N., Green, B. L., Rhoads, K., & Bator, R. (1998). Undermining the undermining effect of reward in sustained interest: When unnecessary conditions are sufficient. *Journal of Applied Social Psychology, 28,* 249–263; Tybout, A. M., & Yalch, R. F. (1980). The effect of experience: A matter of salience? *Journal of Consumer Research, 6,* 406–413.

36. Dweck, C. S. (2006). *Mindset: The new psychology of success.* New York: Ballantine Books.

37. Aronson, E. (1999). The power of self-persuasion. *American Psychologist, 54*(11), 875–884.

38. Milgram, S. (1963). Behavioral study of obedience. *Journal of Abnormal and Social Psychology, 67,* 371–378.

39. Milgram, S. (1974). *Obedience to authority: An experimental view* (p. 6). New York: Harper & Row.

40. Burger, J. M., Messian, N., Patel, S., Prado, A., & Anderson, C. (2004). What coincidence! The effects of incidental similarity on compliance. *Personality and Social Psychology Bulletin, 30,* 35–43.

41. Langer, E. J. (1989). *Mindfulness.* Reading, MA: Addison-Wesley.

42. Kahneman, D. (2011). *Thinking, fast and slow.* New York: Farrar, Straus and Giroux.

43. Mitchell, T. R., Green, S. G., & Wood, R. S. (1982). An attributional model of leadership and the poor subordinate: Development and validation. In B. M. Staw, & L. L. Cummings (Eds.), *Research in organizational behavior* (Vol. 3). Greenwich, CT: SAI Press; Ross, L. (1977). The intuitive psychologist and his shortcomings: Distortions in the attribution process. In L. Berkowitz (Ed.), *Advances in experimental social psychology* (Vol. 10). New York: Academic Press.

44. Heider, F. (1958). *The psychology of interpersonal relations.* New York: Wiley.

45. Mezulis, A. H., Abramson, L. Y., Hyde, J. S., & Hankin, B. L. (2004). Is there a universal positivity bias in attributions? A meta-analytic review of individual, developmental, and cultural differences in the self-serving attributional bias. *Psychological Bulletin, 130*(5), 711–747.

46. Tavris, C., & Wade, C. (1995). *Psychology in perspective.* New York: Harper Collins College Publishers; Wortman, C. B., Loftus, E. F., & Marshall, M. E. (1992). *Psychology* (4th ed.) (Chapter 2). New York: McGraw Hill, Inc.

47. Geller, E. S. (2001). *The psychology of safety handbook* (Chapter 6). Boca Raton, FL: CRC Press.

48. *The American Heritage Dictionary* (1991). Second College Edition. New York: Houghton Mifflin Company, p. 1205.

49. Selye, H. (1974). *Stress without distress* (p. 32). Philadelphia, PA: Lippincott.

50. *The American Heritage Dictionary* (1991). Second College Edition. New York: Houghton Mifflin Company, p. 410.

51. *The New Merriam-Webster Dictionary* (1989). Springfield, MA: Merriam-Webster, Inc., Publishers, p. 224.

52. Geller, E. S. (2018). *Life lessons from psychological science: How to bring the best out of yourself and others.* Plymouth, MI: Macmillan Learning Curriculum Solutions; Geller, E. S., & Geller, K. S. (2017). *Actively caring for people's safety: How to cultivate a brother's/sister's keeper work culture* (pp. 103–104). Park Ridge, IL: American Society of Safety Professionals; Geller, E. S., & Fournier, A. K. (2020). *Actively caring for your child: How to be a more effective parent* (pp. 169–170). Newport, VA: GellerAC4P, Inc.

53. Carver, C. S., Scheier, M. F., & Weintraub, J. K. (1989). Assessing coping strategies: A theoretically-based approach. *Journal of Personality and Social Psychology, 56,* 267–283.

54. Scheier, M. F., Weintraub, J. K., & Carver, C. S. (1986). Coping with stress: Divergent strategies of optimists and pessimists. *Journal of Personality and Social Psychology, 51,* 1257–1264.

55. Bryant, F. B., & Cvengros, J. S. (2004). Distinguishing hope and optimism: Two sides of a coin, or two separate coins? *Journal of Social and Clinical Psychology, 23*(2), 273–302.

56. Friedman, M., & Ulmar, D. (1984). *Treating Type A behavior and your heart.* New York: Knopf; Rhodewalt, F., & Smith, T. W. (1991). Current issues in Type A behavior, coronary proneness, and coronary heart disease. In C. R. Snyder & D. R. Forsyth (Eds.), *Handbook of social and clinical psychology.* New York: Pergamon Press.

57. Chida, Y., & Hamer, M. (2008). Chronic psychosocial factors and acute physiological responses to laboratory-induced stress in healthy populations: A quantitative review of 30 years of investigation. *Psychological Bulletin, 134,* 829–885; Chida, Y., & Steptoe, A. (2009). The association of anger and hostility with future coronary heart disease: A meta-analytic review of prospective evidence. *Journal of the American College of Cardiology, 17,* 936–946.

58. Geller, E. S. (2008). *Leading people-based safety: Enriching your culture* (pp. 131–134). Virginia Beach, VA: Coastal Training Technologies Corporation.

59. Gray, J. (1992). *Men are from Mars, women are from Venus.* New York: Harper Collins.

60. Myers, I. B., & McCaulley, M. H. (1985). *Manual: A guide to the development and use of the Myers-Briggs Type Indicator.* Palo Alto, CA: Consulting Psychologists Press.

61. Birkman, R. W. (1995). *True colors: Get to know yourself and others better.* New York: Thomas Nelson Inc.; Kalil, C. (2013). *Follow your true colors to the work you love* (13th ed.). New York: Dreammaker Publishing; Kalil, C., & Lowery, D. (1991). *Follow your true colors to the work you love: The workbook: A journey in self-discovery & career decision-making.* New York: Incorporated Publishing; Kiersey, D. (1998). *Please understand me II: Temperament, character, intelligence.* Del Mar, CA: Prometheus Nemesis Book Company; Maddron, T. (1995). *Living your colors: Practical wisdom for life, love, work, and play.* New York: Warner Books, Inc; Ritberger, C. (2009). *What color is your personality? Red, orange, yellow, green.* New York: Hay House, Inc.

62. Krisco, K. H. (1997). *Leadership and the art of conversation.* Rocklin, CA: Prima; Geller, E. S. (2016). Effective AC4P communication. In E. S. Geller (Ed.), *Applied psychology: Actively caring for people* (pp. 153–184). New York: Cambridge University Press.

63. Geller, E. S. (2002). *The participation factor: How to increase involvement in occupational safety* (pp. 180–187). Des Plaines, IL: American Society of Safety Engineers.

64. *The American Heritage Dictionary* (1991). Second College Edition. New York: Houghton Mifflin Company, p. 233.

65. James, W. (1890). *The principles of psychology* (Vol. 2). New York: Holt; Schacter, S., & Singer, J. E. (1962). Cognitive, social and physiological determinants of emotional state. *Psychological Review, 69*, 379–399.

66. Laird, J. D. (1974). Self-attribution of emotions: The effects of expressive behavior on the quality of emotional experience. *Journal of Personality and Social Psychology, 29*, 475–486.

67. Havas, D. A., Glenberg, A. M., & Rink, M. (2007). Emotion stimulation during language comprehension. *Psychometric Bulletin Review, 14*, 436–441; Myers, D. G. (2013). *Psychology* (10th ed.) (Chapter 12). New York: Worth Publishers.

68. Lerner, M. J. (1980). *The belief in a just world: A fundamental delusion.* New York: Plenum.

69. Aronson, E., Wilson, T. D., & Akert, R. M. (1998). *Social psychology* (3rd ed.). New York: Addison Wesley Longman, Inc.

70. Maslow, A. H. (1971). *The farther reaches of human nature.* New York: Viking.

ACKNOWLEDGEMENTS

For more than 40 years, I've taught Actively-Caring-for-People (AC4P) principles and applications in workshops and keynote addresses at regional and national conferences, as well as at various Fortune 500 companies. The evidence-based AC4P lessons have always been well-received. However, my evaluations have periodically included a critical comment such as, "I appreciate the theory and principles presented but I don't know how to apply Dr. Geller's lessons."

This LifeCOACH manual addresses this legitimate concern in the best way possible. How? By combining introductions to 50 research-based principles from psychological science with relevant illustrations and discussion questions to engage participants in constructive conversations about specific ways to apply each life lesson for the benefit of human well-being.

First, I'm pleased to acknowledge the creator of the instructive and entertaining illustrations that introduce each life lesson. Since 1990, my teaching, textbooks, and workbooks have benefited from the artistry of George V. Wills. Thank you, George—your illustrations inspired me to write this LifeCOACH manual, and I expect them to facilitate the teaching and learning from this scholarship.

Next, I acknowledge the 30+-year friendship and support of John W. Drebinger Jr. As a leading "motivational teacher" for occupational health and safety, John has given me invaluable feedback for continuously improving my professional presentations. He created and launched the AC4P website—www.ac4p. org—which provides foundational resources for the worldwide AC4P Movement, including inspirational AC4P stories, the AC4P theme song, related verbal presentations, research-based scholarship, and practical materials to support an ongoing and large-scale AC4P process.

I also acknowledge the education/training and consultancy of Safety Performance Solutions, Inc. (www.safetyperformance.com)—its team of partners, my collaborators, who have been teaching the AC4P principles and applications covered in this LifeCOACH manual to organizations worldwide since 1993. Indeed, this organization has verified the real-world applied benefits of the contents of this scholarship by using the AC4P principles to reduce the injury rates of numerous companies worldwide for more than 25 years.

Plus, I am extremely grateful for the dedication of numerous Virginia Tech students and associates in our University Center for Applied Behavior Systems (CABS). Since its foundation in 1987, students and colleagues in CABS have collected and analyzed endless streams of field data to test the impact of various AC4P interventions, and thereby inform the design of more effective ways to increase the frequency and improve the quality of AC4P behavior.

The support system of CABS serves as a "think tank" for considering innovative approaches to improve the human dynamics of interpersonal relations and enhance the large-scale impact of the AC4P Movement. In this regard, I am particularly beholden to my current graduate students: Nick Flannery, Trevin Glasgow, Zack Mastrich, and Jack Wardale; our CABS Coordinator for the 2019–2020 academic year, Jordan Oliver; and our research scientist, Dr. Erica Feuerbacher.

My 50-year teaching and research career at Virginia Tech, reflected by much of the contents in this LifeCOACH manual, has benefited dramatically from an extensive support system in both the academic and consulting worlds—professional colleagues, university students, and consumers of my books and education/training programs. All of you have offered supportive and corrective feedback to help me improve, and you've inspired me to keep on keeping on. You continually remind me of Life Lesson 50—*The Legacy of Teaching and Learning*.

Speaking of legacy, my Number 1 inspiration has been my daughter—Krista S. Geller. From high school and throughout college and graduate school, Krista was a dedicated research assistant in CABS, and her master's thesis and PhD dissertation studied the value of pets as AC4P agents. In fact, Krista summarized this innovative research in the final chapter of the 700-word textbook published by Cambridge University Press: *Applied Psychology: Actively Caring for People*.

Needless to say, Krista has been intimately connected with the AC4P principles revealed in this LifeCOACH manual for most of her life, and she has recently begun teaching these life lessons to organizations nationwide as President of our new co-founded education/training and consulting firm—GellerAC4P, Inc.

Finally, I am very appreciative of the invaluable collaboration with the Cognella support staff, from Clare Kennedy's initial recognition of the teaching/learning potential of this scholarship to the productive vision and leadership of Tony Paese and the creative developmental support of Susana Christie. Evidence-based knowledge cannot make a difference without an accepted, attractive, and appreciated presentation for large-scale dissemination. Thank you, Cognella, for making this possible.

Thank you all so very much. The synergy from your past, present, and future sustenance enables a legacy—AC4P life lessons that readers can use to enrich their lives and contribute to cultivating cultures of interpersonal compassion and AC4P behavior at work, at school, at home, and in every other context where the science of human experience can inspire AC4P behavior and enhance human well-being.

ABOUT THE AUTHOR

E. Scott Geller, Ph.D., an Alumni Distinguished Professor at Virginia Tech, is co-founder and senior partner of Safety Performance Solutions, Inc., a leading-edge training and consulting organization specializing in behavior-based safety since 1995 (safetyperformance.com), and co-founder of GellerAC4P, a consulting/training firm dedicated to teaching and spreading the Actively Caring for People (AC4P) Movement worldwide (www.gellerac4p.org). For five decades, Professor Geller has taught and conducted research as a faculty member and Director of the Center for Applied Behavior Systems in the Department of Psychology at Virginia Tech.

He has authored, edited, or co-authored 49 books, 88 book chapters, 39 training programs, 270 magazine articles, and more than 300 research articles addressing the development and evaluation of behavior-focused interventions to improve quality of life on a large scale. His most recent textbook, with 31 co-authors, *Applied Psychology: Actively Caring for People*, defines Dr. Geller's research, teaching, and scholarship career at Virginia Tech, which epitomizes the Virginia Tech logo: *Ut Prosim*— "That I May Serve."

His popular books in applied psychology include: *The Psychology of Safety: Improving Behaviors and Attitudes on the Job; Working Safe: How to Help People Actively Care for Health and Safety; Understanding Behavior-Based Safety; Building Successful Safety Teams; Beyond Safety Accountability: How to Increase Personal*

Responsibility; The Psychology of Safety Handbook; Keys to Behavior-Based Safety from Safety Performance Solutions; The Participation Factor: How to Increase Involvement in Occupational Safety; People-Based Safety: The Source; People-Based Patient Safety: Enriching Your Culture to Prevent Medical Error, co-authored with Dave Johnson; *Leading People-Based Safety: Enriching Your Culture; Life Lessons from Psychological Science: How to Bring the Best out of Yourself and Others; Actively Caring at Your School: How to Make It Happen; The Courage to Actively Care: How to Cultivate a Culture of Interpersonal Compassion* and *The Motivation to Actively Care: How You Can Make It Happen,* both co-authored with Bob Veazie; *Actively Caring for People Policing: Building Positive Police/Citizen Relations,* co-authored with Bobby Kipper; *Actively Caring for People in Schools: How to Cultivate a Culture of Compassion; 50 Lessons to Enrich Your Life: Proven Principles from Psychological Science; Actively Caring for People's Safety: How to Cultivate a Brother's/Sister's Keeper Work Culture,* co-authored with Krista S. Geller; and *Actively Caring for Your Child: How to Be a More Effective Parent,* co-authored with Angela Fournier.

Dr. Geller is a Fellow of the American Psychological Association, the Association for Psychological Science, the Association of Behavior Analysis International, and the World Academy of Productivity and Quality Sciences. He is past Editor of the *Journal of Applied Behavior Analysis* (1989–1992), Associate Editor of *Environment and Behavior* (1982–2017), and current Consulting Editor for *Behavior and Social Issues,* the *Journal of Organizational Behavior Management,* and the *Journal of Safety Research.*

Dr. Geller has been the principal investigator for more than 75 research grants totaling more than $7 million in extramural support to design, implement, and evaluate behavioral science interventions for the benefit of corporations, institutions, government agencies, and communities at large. Both government agencies and corporations have funded his research including: the National Science Foundation; the National Institute for Occupational Safety and Health; the U.S. Department of Health, Education, and Welfare; the U.S. Department of Energy; the U.S. Department of Transportation; the U.S. Department of Justice; the National Highway Traffic Safety Administration; the National Institute on Alcohol Abuse and Alcoholism; the Centers for Disease Control and Prevention; Ford Motor Company, General Motors Research Laboratories; the Alcoholic Beverage Medical Research Foundation; and the Virginia Departments of Energy, Transportation, Litter Control, Agriculture and Commerce, and Welfare and Institutions.

Scott Geller's dedication, talent, and energy have helped him earn a teaching award in 1982 from the American Psychological Association and every university teaching award offered at Virginia Tech. Moreover, in 2001 Virginia Tech awarded Dr. Geller the University Alumni Award for Excellence in Research. In 2002, the University honored him with the Alumni Outreach Award for his exemplary real-world applications of behavioral science, and in 2003 he received the University Alumni Award for Graduate Student Advising. In 2005, he was awarded the statewide Virginia Outstanding Faculty Award by the State Council of Higher Education, and Virginia Tech conferred the title of Alumni Distinguished Professor on him.

Dr. Geller has received lifetime achievement awards from the International Organizational Behavior Management Network (in 2008) and the American Psychological Foundation (in 2009). In 2010 he was honored with the Outstanding Applied Research Award from the American Psychological Association's Division of Applied Behavior Analysis, and in 2019 Professor Geller received the APA Division 25 Nathan H. Azrin Distinguished Contributions to Applied Behavior Analysis Award. In 2011, the College of Wooster awarded E. Scott Geller the honorary degree: Doctor of Humane Letters.